CONVECTION OVEN COOKBOOK

Other Books by Carmel Berman Reingold

COOKBOOKS

The Crockery Pot Cookbook
Cuisinart: Food Processor Cooking

NONFICTION

Remarriage
How to Be Happy If You Marry Again
Bible Therapy

FICTION

The Last Carnival

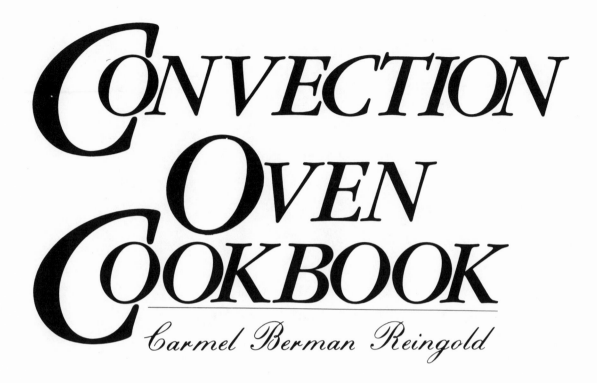

CONVECTION OVEN COOKBOOK

Carmel Berman Reingold

LIPPINCOTT & CROWELL, PUBLISHERS

New York

FIRST EDITION

Designer: C. Linda Dingler

Library of Congress Cataloging in Publication Data

Reingold, Carmel Berman.
  Convection oven cookbook.

  Includes index.
  1. Convection oven cookery. I. Title.
TX840.C65R44 1980   641.5′8   80–7859
ISBN 0–690–01980–7
ISBN 0–690–01982–3 (pbk.)

80 81 82 83 84 10 9 8 7 6 5 4 3 2 1

CONTENTS

Thanks to. . .

. . . all the guests and members of my family who tried the various dishes that I prepared in the six convection ovens I worked with. I particularly appreciate my husband Harry Reingold's patience when faced one evening with six pumpkin pies and twenty-four hamburgers—one pie and four hamburgers per oven.

I'm also grateful to the professional chefs who showed me how convection ovens were used in their wonderful restaurant kitchens, especially Chef Seppi of the Four Seasons Restaurant in New York City and Herb McCarthy of the Bowden Square Restaurant in Southampton, Long Island.

In France, where convection ovens have been longer in home use than here, I want to thank Batia Feldman and Claudie Danziger of Paris for sharing some of their favorite recipes with me.

And my special thanks to Gail Piazza, a most talented home economist, for her assistance in helping me test the recipes in this book.

1
A New Way of Cooking: The Convection Oven

For more than twenty years, restaurant chefs and commercial bakers have been relying on a special piece of equipment—the convection oven—for the preparation of a wide range of foods, including breads, pizzas, and meats of all kinds. Professional cooks know that these ovens can roast a duck to crispy brown perfection, broil a lobster so that it comes out tender and moist, and bake a number of trays of cookies at one time—each cookie a crisp, golden mouthful.

Now, finally, as with the food processor, the convection oven has come home. At this time, there are six countertop convection ovens available for the home cook who wants to save time, conserve energy, and yet present guests and family with delicious meals.

How does the convection oven work? Very simply, heat is circulated constantly around the food in the oven. A fan conveys air that is temperature controlled, and because all the surfaces of the food—be it a chicken, a roast, or a hamburger—are exposed to the same heat, the food is succulently brown all over, while remaining moist and juicy within.

SAVE MONEY . . . SAVE ENERGY

• You can roast, broil, and bake in convection ovens. In some ovens you can also slow-cook, dehydrate, and cook on a special shish kebab accessory, or barbecue on a rotisserie.

• Because hot air circulates constantly around the food as it cooks, you save time—frequently as much as one-third when compared with conventional ovens.

• You save energy when cooking the convection way. Foods need less time in a convection oven and can be cooked at a temperature 20 to 75 degrees lower than in a conventional oven.

• Figures from various groups testing convection ovens have differed, but the savings in cost are approximately one-third compared with the average electric oven, and even more when compared with a gas oven—when you save energy, you save money.

• With heat swirling about the food from all sides, you no longer have to turn hamburgers or steak. They will cook evenly—and beautifully—both top and bottom.

• Though the convection oven is smaller than a conventional oven, it can cook a whole meal at one time. That's because with a convection oven you don't have to worry about centering that pie, or putting the chicken on the middle rack. The circulating hot air keeps the temperature nearly the same throughout the oven.

• Thanks to that circulating hot air, you can cook entrees and desserts at the same time. Flavors and odors do not transfer from one food to another when you're convection cooking.

• Convection cooking is convenient. A convection oven can cook a simple roast, or impress everyone with a high-rising soufflé.

Save time, energy, money, and cook deliciously—that's the exciting message of convection cooking.

CONVECTION vs. CONVENTIONAL vs. MICROWAVE COOKING

All appliances have their advocates and all appliances have their plus and minus sides. One research group tested three convection ovens against their top-rated self-cleaning electric range, and found the convection ovens wanting.

Truth to be told, though, not many kitchens come equipped with the top-rated oven, and the convection oven compares favorably with, and often scores higher than, the average ovens found in most homes and apartments.

People we spoke to who owned both convection and conventional ovens said that once they became thoroughly acquainted with the way their convection ovens worked, they used them more often than their conventional ovens. They liked the time-saving aspect of the convection oven, and more than that, they liked the delicious results.

No appliance can match the microwave oven for speed. However, most microwave ovens just can not deliver the brown, crusty roasts and steaks that come from a convection oven. In addition, here is something that microwave devotees forget to mention: quantity of food counts when cooking in a microwave oven. If one potato takes 5 minutes to microwave, ten potatoes take ten times as long. But you can put ten potatoes in a convection oven and the time remains the same—45 minutes for all ten potatoes.

There is nothing mysterious about convection cooking—you don't have to take a course in physics if you want to know how a convection oven works. It's temperature-controlled hot air circulating constantly within an oven to cook food to juicy perfection, and there are no microwaves to worry about.

THE RIGHT CONVECTION OVEN FOR YOU

Countertop convection ovens come in a variety of sizes and shapes, and some have additional, optional functions and features. If you haven't bought your oven as yet, take a look at the full range of convection ovens before buying.

Here are points to look for:

• Size and shape. Is the convection oven going to be your only oven, or is it your second oven? How large a roast or turkey do you want to cook? Some ovens are larger than others. One can be wall mounted. Measure your counter and wall space before buying. One oven is small, portable, and easy to store—a good possibility for a weekend or summer home.

• Do you plan to slow-cook in the convection oven? Some of the ovens are equipped for slow cooking, which means that a stew, casserole, or pot roast can cook all day while you're away from home. If this is important to you, make sure that the convection oven you're buying has this feature.

• At this time, one oven comes with a rotisserie, while another comes with a special rack and skewers for shish kebab. These features enable you to have barbecue-type meals all winter long.

• Dehydrating. If you have a kitchen garden and grow your own herbs, or if you have a larger garden full of summertime tomatoes, apples, or onions, take a look at the convection ovens that come with the accessories for dehydrating. These ovens operate at the low temperature necessary for proper dehydration and have a thermostat control that allows the oven to remain on for hours.

• Some ovens are continuously self-cleaning, and some have built-in meat thermometers. One oven has a timer that will turn the oven on—good if you want a roast or a casserole to start cooking while you're away from home.

• Insulation. In general, kitchens remain cooler when any convection oven is used because the cooking time needed is less and the temperature is lower, but if you want to keep really cool, take a look at the models that offer extra insulation.

• Extra racks and cookie sheets can be purchased for some ovens.

WHEN YOU COOK BY CONVECTION

You've chosen the convection oven that's right for your kitchen and life style. Now this wonderful appliance is in your home, and you're eager to use it.

Before you do anything, read the manufacturer's instructions!

The convection oven is not a gadget or a toy, it is an electrical appliance, and as such it has definite dos and don'ts. To be perfectly informed about these, *do* read the book that comes with your oven.

Some important tips to remember:

• The convection oven needs no special wiring or installation; one oven uses a three-prong plug. Always follow the manufacturer's directions on how much space to leave around the back and/or sides of the oven.

• If your oven comes with a removable top, make sure you have left space on your counter where you can place that top.

• Don't be super neat and decide to cover the racks of your convection oven with foil—this will prevent the heat from circulating around the food.

• If your convection oven doesn't come with a built-in meat thermometer, use a meat thermometer of your own, at least until you become familiar with the way the oven works. Remember, though, that as with any other oven a roast will keep cooking for a few minutes after you've removed it from the oven.

• You don't need special pots or pans for a convection oven. Any ovenproof vessel that fits in your oven will do. However, dark metal is a better conductor of heat than glass, and food in a shallow dish will cook faster than food in a deep dish.

• Foods go from freezer to oven without preheating. If using convenience foods, follow package directions and bake according to suggested temperatures, but check for doneness approximately 10 minutes before suggested time.

• Most recipes do not call for preheating. However, some manufacturers recommend preheating for certain roasts and broiled meats. Check the use and care book that came with your oven before adapting your own recipes.

• Don't connect your convection oven on the same circuit or outlet where you're already working with other appliances. This is especially important to remember in the summer, when some utility companies reduce the voltage coming into the home, in order to avoid an overload of the electrical system.

• Get to know your oven. Once you do, you'll be able to adapt your own favorite recipes to convection cooking.

• In general, when roasting, start out by reducing the oven temperature 30 degrees and the cooking time by one-third. Until you're thoroughly familiar with your oven, check 5 to 10 minutes before the end of the suggested cooking time.

• Don't touch hot surfaces. Use door handles and control knobs, and be careful when removing a drip pan that contains hot cooking juices or grease.

THE CONVECTION OVEN MEAL PLAN

Now that you own a convection oven, use it to its fullest capacity to create a delicious, energy-saving, money-saving dinner. You can cook more than one course at a time in your oven. There's no problem about centering the food, because oven temperatures remain constant in all parts of the oven, and there's no worry about food odors moving from one dish to another—the circulating hot air takes care of that.

2
APPETIZERS AND FIRST COURSES

APPETIZERS AND FIRST COURSES

Toasted Almonds Saratoga

Roast Chestnuts

Eggplant Caviar

Cabbage Strudel

Easy Brandied Pâté

Pâté en Croûte

Pâté de Campagne

Pâté of Goose with Pistachios

Olive Tarta Español

South American Empañadas

Party Sausage Quiches

French Onion Tart

Curried Crescents

Spicy Beef in a Blanket

Baked Stuffed Mushrooms

Baked Stuffed Clams

Sponge Roll with Chicken Mornay

Ham Puffs

Potato-Cheese Puffs

There are many people who would happily make an entire meal of a variety of delicious appetizers. The convection oven is especially pleasing at party time, because you can heat tray after tray of hors d'oeuvre quickly and without fuss, muss, or overheating your kitchen.

If you have prepared appetizers in advance and frozen them, take them directly from the freezer and place them in your convection oven. No preheating is necessary.

If you wish, you can cook or heat an appetizer, such as the Olive Tarta Español on page 15, while at the same time cooking an entree—Cantonese Pork with Stir-Fried Vegetables (page 67), for example.

TOASTED ALMONDS SARATOGA

Don't overlook this recipe, thinking it's too simple to be interesting. Serve the almonds to guests and hear them say, "How do you do these? They're marvelous!" You can look mysteriously into the middle distance, if you wish, because no one will believe how easy it was.

2 cups whole, blanched almonds
4 teaspoons vegetable oil
Salt to taste (optional)

Place the almonds in a flat, ovenproof pan that will contain them in one layer. Spoon the oil over and convection-bake in a 300-degree oven for 10 to 15 minutes, or until the almonds are a light brown.

Salt or not, as you wish.

Serves: 4 to 8

ROAST CHESTNUTS

Roast chestnuts are a European and English favorite. Serve them with a dry wine as an appetizer, or with a sweet sherry or Marsala for dessert.

1 pound chestnuts

Working carefully, cut a cross in each of the shells of 1 pound of chestnuts. Place the chestnuts in one layer in a shallow, ovenproof dish and convection-bake in a 350-degree oven for 20 to 30 minutes, or until tender.

Serves: 6

EGGPLANT CAVIAR

This spicy eggplant dish is perfect as a first course, or makes a delicious appetizer served with wine, cocktails, or tomato juice. Eggplant caviar may be spread on crackers or served with a fork.

1 large eggplant
1 onion, peeled and diced
1 green pepper, seeded and diced
1 tomato, peeled and chopped
Juice of ½ lemon
½ cup olive oil
Salt and freshly ground black pepper to taste
¼ teaspoon Tabasco or hot pepper sauce (optional)

Pierce the eggplant in a few places with a sharp knife. Place the eggplant on a rack and convection-bake at Maximum temperature, or until the skin is charred and the eggplant is soft to the touch. The eggplant should be cooked in 20 to 30 minutes, depending on its size.

Allow the eggplant to cool, and then peel. Cut the peeled eggplant in half and drain off any liquid, then chop the pulp into a coarse puree. Place in bowl and stir in all other ingredients, combining thoroughly.

Chill before serving.

Serves: 4 to 6

CABBAGE STRUDEL

Strudel does not have to mean dessert. It can also double as an interesting appetizer, when a spicy cabbage mixture is used as a filling for the delicate, crisp pastry. Using packaged strudel or phyllo dough makes this dish much easier to prepare.

FILLING

2 pounds cabbage
Salt
¼ pound (1 stick) butter
2 tablespoons granulated sugar
Freshly ground black pepper to taste

DOUGH

2 sheets of packaged strudel or phyllo dough
¼ cup melted butter
¼ cup fine breadcrumbs

Prepare the filling first. Shred the cabbage and sprinkle lightly with salt. Place the salted cabbage in a bowl and allow to stand for an hour. At the end of that time, squeeze the cabbage by handfuls, eliminating the water that has been drawn out by the salt. Rinse well and squeeze again.

Heat half the butter in a large skillet. Add half the cabbage and 1 tablespoon of the sugar. Stir-fry until the cabbage is a golden brown. Remove the cooked cabbage to a bowl and repeat with the remaining cabbage.

When all the cabbage is cooked and in the bowl, add black pepper and stir. The mixture is supposed to be spicy.

Preheat the convection oven to 350 degrees for 5 to 10 minutes.

Prepare the strudel or phyllo dough according to package directions. Spread half the melted butter over one sheet of strudel dough and sprinkle with half the breadcrumbs. Place the second sheet of strudel dough over the first and repeat with the remaining butter and crumbs.

Spread the cooked cabbage along one long side of the strudel dough, and roll as you would a jelly roll. Place the strudel in a baking pan, and convection-bake for 15 to 20 minutes, or until the strudel is golden.

Serves: 6 to 8

A WEALTH OF PÂTÉS

Pâtés are not as difficult to make as you may think. Some do call for ingredients that may be hard to find, but others are as simple to prepare as a meat loaf. Indeed, if you think of pâtés as a more interesting form of baked meat loaf, you'll try making your own.

The four recipes that follow include an easy pâté made with brandy, as well as an authentic country-style pâté and a pâté baked in a crust. Try the Easy Brandied Pâté first if you've never baked a pâté before, and after your success with that, go on to the other recipes.

EASY BRANDIED PÂTÉ

2 pounds lean pork, ground
1 pound pork liver, ground
¼ pound chicken livers, ground
¾ pound pork fat, ground
2 teaspoons salt
½ teaspoon green peppercorns
¼ teaspoon dried thyme
½ cup brandy
2 bay leaves

Combine all the ground meats and the fat and mix thoroughly. Add all the other ingredients, except for the bay leaves, and mix thoroughly once again.

Cook a spoonful of the mixture in a skillet. Make sure it's thoroughly cooked, and then taste. Correct the seasoning.

Butter a 2½-quart ovenproof casserole and turn the pâté mixture into it. Top the pâté with the bay leaves. Cover the casserole and convection-bake in a 350-degree oven for 1½ hours, or until a meat thermometer registers 140 degrees.

Remove the cover and bake for an additional 30 minutes, or until the thermometer registers 170 to 175 degrees.

Cool and chill before serving.

Serves: Approximately 12

PÂTÉ EN CROÛTE

PASTRY

2¾ cups all-purpose flour
½ teaspoon salt
½ pound (2 sticks) butter
4–5 tablespoons ice water, approximately

PÂTÉ

2 pounds chicken livers, ground
½ pound ground beef
½ pound lean pork, ground
2 eggs
2 tablespoons Cognac or brandy
1 onion, peeled and chopped
1 clove garlic, peeled and mashed
¾ cup heavy sweet cream
¾ cup all-purpose flour
2 teaspoons salt
½ teaspoon ground ginger
½ teaspoon freshly ground black pepper
½ teaspoon ground allspice

Prepare the pastry first. In a small mixing bowl, combine the flour and salt. Cut the butter into the flour, using a pastry blender or two knives, until the particles are the size of small peas. Sprinkle water over the flour mixture, 1 tablespoon at a time, and stir with a fork until the dough is lightly moistened. Form into a ball and refrigerate for 30 minutes.

Combine all the pâté ingredients and blend thoroughly, using an electric mixer or a food processor. Cook a spoonful of the mixture thoroughly in a skillet, taste, and add more seasonings if necessary.

Roll out the pastry on a lightly floured board, forming an 18 × 12-inch rectangle. Fit the pastry into a 6-cup ovenproof terrine. Or, if you prefer, use two small pans having a combined capacity of 6 cups. There should be enough additional pastry, after the pan or pans are lined, to cover the top of the pâté.

Turn the pâté into the pastry-lined pan and fold the pastry over the top of the pâté, sealing well. Form a rosette with dough scraps and place in the center of the pastry. Pierce a hole through the center of rosette, to allow steam to escape.

Convection-bake the pâté at 350 degrees for 1 hour and 20 minutes to 1 hour and 30 minutes, or until the pastry is golden brown and a meat thermometer registers 170 to 175 degrees.

Allow to cool for 4 to 5 hours before refrigerating.

Serves: 18

PÂTÉ DE CAMPAGNE

½ pound lean pork, finely ground
½ pound veal or chicken, finely ground
½ pound fresh pork fat, finely ground
1 tablespoon salt
½ teaspoon ground allspice
½ teaspoon dried thyme
1 clove garlic, peeled and mashed
2 tablespoons brandy
2 eggs
½ cup minced onion, sautéed in butter
¾ pound pork, beef, or calf's liver, cut
 into ½-inch dice
Sheets of fresh pork fat, ⅛ inch thick (may
 be fatback, or fat from loin of pork
 roast, or blanched salt pork), to line
 the terrine and to cover the meat
1 bay leaf

Using an electric mixer or food processor, beat together the ground meats, fat, seasonings, garlic, brandy, eggs, and onion. Blend thoroughly. Thoroughly cook a spoonful of the mixture in a skillet, taste, and add more seasonings if necessary. Fold in the diced liver.

Cut sheets of pork fat to line a 6-cup terrine, oven-proof baking dish, or 9 × 5 × 3-inch loaf pan. Press the pork fat sheets against the bottom and sides of the pan.

Turn the meat mixture into the pan. Smooth the surface and place the bay leaf on top. Cover with a final sheet of pork fat and press aluminum foil over and around the edges of the pan to enclose the meat completely.

Convection-bake in a 325-degree oven for 1 hour and 40 minutes to 2 hours. The pâté is done when it has begun to shrink from the sides of the pan and the rendered fat is clear yellow with no trace of pink-colored juices. A meat thermometer should read 170 to 175 degrees.

Cool the pâté and refrigerate overnight. Serve chilled.

Serves: 12 to 16

PÂTÉ OF GOOSE WITH PISTACHIOS

½ pound pork liver, finely ground
½ pound lean pork, finely ground
1 goose breast, boned, skinned and finely ground
½ pound bacon, finely ground
2 eggs
2 tablespoons all-purpose flour
1 cup dry white wine
2 ounces shallots, peeled and chopped
2 ounces shelled pistachio nuts
Salt and freshly ground black pepper to taste
¼ pound sliced bacon

Using an electric mixer or food processor, beat together the ground meats and ground bacon with all other ingredients, except for the remaining ¼ pound of sliced bacon.

Sauté 1 tablespoon of the mixture in a small skillet until thoroughly cooked. Taste and correct the seasoning.

Line a 9 × 5 × 3-inch loaf pan with the remaining bacon slices. Turn the pâté mixture into the loaf pan and cover the pan with foil, sealing tightly. Place the loaf pan in another, larger pan and pour hot water into the second pan.

Convection-bake in a 325-degree oven for 1 hour and 40 minutes, or until a meat thermometer registers 170 to 175 degrees.

Cool, then refrigerate for 24 hours before serving.

Serves: 8

OLIVE TARTA ESPAÑOL

1 9-inch pie shell, partially baked (see page 125)
1 tablespoon grated Parmesan cheese
3 slices bacon
1 small onion, peeled and sliced
2 teaspoons all-purpose flour
1 cup light cream
2 eggs
¼ cup milk
⅓ cup chopped stuffed green olives
2 tablespoons chopped fresh parsley
Salt and freshly ground black pepper to taste

Sprinkle the partially baked pie crust with the Parmesan cheese and set aside.

Fry the bacon in a large skillet. Drain, crumble, and set aside. Sauté the onion in the bacon drippings until translucent. Stir in the flour and cook an additional 2 minutes. Add the light cream to the skillet and cook, stirring, until slightly thickened.

Beat the eggs with the milk and stir in the olives, parsley, and salt and pepper. Pour gradually into the skillet, stirring to combine. Add the crumbled bacon.

Pour the contents of the skillet into the pie shell and convection-bake in a 325-degree oven for 25 to 30 minutes, or until a knife inserted in the center comes out dry.

Serve warm.

Serves: 10

SOUTH AMERICAN EMPAÑADAS

PASTRY

2¼ cups all-purpose flour
¼ teaspoon salt
6 ounces (1½ sticks) butter
4 to 5 tablespoons ice water,
    approximately

FILLING

½ pound ground beef
1 medium onion, peeled and chopped
1 clove garlic, peeled and mashed
1 tablespoon vegetable oil
1 teaspoon chili powder
¼ teaspoon ground cumin
½ teaspoon salt
1 teaspoon Worcestershire sauce
1 cup stewed tomatoes
¼ cup chopped raisins
2 tablespoons chopped green olives

Prepare the pastry first. In a small mixing bowl, combine the flour and salt. Cut the butter into the flour, using a pastry blender or two knives, until the particles are the size of small peas. Sprinkle ice water over the flour mixture, 1 tablespoon at a time, until the dough is moistened. Mix with a fork, then form into a ball and refrigerate for 30 minutes.

Sauté the meat, onion, and garlic in the oil until lightly brown. Add the remaining ingredients and simmer for about 20 minutes, stirring from time to time.

Preheat the convection oven to 400 degrees for 5 to 10 minutes.

On a floured board, roll the dough into an 18 × 14-inch rectangle. Cut the dough into 2-inch circles. Spoon approximately ½ teaspoonful of the meat mixture into the center of each dough circle. Fold over and seal the edges well.

Place the *empañadas* on an unbuttered cookie sheet and convection-bake for 8 to 10 minutes, or until they are a light brown.

Yield: 40 to 48 empañadas

PARTY SAUSAGE QUICHES

PASTRY

2¼ cups all-purpose flour
 ½ teaspoon salt
 6 ounces (1½ sticks) butter
 4 to 5 tablespoons ice water,
     approximately

FILLING

 1 medium onion, peeled and chopped
 2 tablespoons butter
 ½ pound pork sausage meat
 1 tablespoon chopped fresh parsley
 ½ teaspoon salt
 ½ teaspoon freshly ground black pepper
 5 eggs
1½ cups light cream
 ¾ cup grated mozzarella cheese
 ¾ cup grated Gruyère cheese
 1 tablespoon freshly grated Parmesan
     cheese
 1 tablespoon all-purpose flour

Prepare the pastry first. In a small mixing bowl, combine the flour and salt. Cut the butter into flour, using a pastry blender or two knives, until the particles are the size of small peas. Sprinkle ice water over the flour mixture, 1 tablespoon at a time, and stir with a fork until the dough is lightly moistened. Form into a ball and refrigerate for 30 minutes.

Sauté the onion in the butter until limp, then add the sausage meat, parsley, salt, and pepper and brown thoroughly.

Combine all the other ingredients in a large bowl, beating thoroughly. Stir in the sausage mixture.

Divide the dough into 12 parts, and roll each piece out on a floured board. Fit the pieces of dough into standard 3½-inch tart pans. Stir the sausage-egg mixture and put approximately ⅓ cup of it into each tart pan.

Convection-bake the quiches in a 325-degree oven for 20 to 25 minutes, or until a knife inserted in the center comes out dry.

Yield: 12 individual quiches

FRENCH ONION TART

PASTRY

1⅓ cups all-purpose flour
¼ teaspoon salt
¼ pound (1 stick) butter
2 to 3 tablespoons ice water

FILLING

¼ pound (1 stick) butter
4 medium onions, peeled and thinly
   sliced
½ teaspoon salt
¼ teaspoon freshly ground white pepper
5 eggs, lightly beaten
1½ cups light cream
1 tablespoon freshly grated Parmesan
   cheese
1 tablespoon all-purpose flour

Prepare the pastry first. In a small mixing bowl, combine the flour and salt. Cut butter into flour with a pastry blender or two knives until particles are the size of small peas. Sprinkle ice water, 1 tablespoonful at a time, over flour mixture, tossing with a fork until dough is slightly moist. Form dough into a ball and refrigerate for 30 minutes.

Sauté onions in butter, stirring, until onions are translucent. Combine onions with all other ingredients, mixing well.

Roll out dough on a lightly floured board and fit into a 9-inch pie plate.

Pour onion-egg mixture into crust.

Convection-bake in a 325-degree oven for 20 to 25 minutes, or until a knife inserted 1 inch from center comes out dry.

Serves: 10

CURRIED CRESCENTS

PASTRY

2¼ cups all-purpose flour
 ½ teaspoon salt
 6 ounces (1½ sticks) butter
 4 to 5 tablespoons ice water,
   approximately

FILLING

 ¼ pound lean pork, ground
 1 clove garlic, peeled and mashed
 ¼ cup chopped green onions
 1 tablespoon vegetable oil
 1 tablespoon soy sauce
 1 tablespoon dry sherry
 ½ teaspoon curry powder
 ½ teaspoon salt
 2 teaspoons brown sugar
 1 large potato, peeled, boiled, and
   mashed
 1 egg, lightly beaten

Prepare the pastry first. In a small mixing bowl, combine the flour and salt. Cut the butter into the flour, using a pastry blender or two knives, until the particles are the size of small peas. Sprinkle ice water over the flour mixture, 1 tablespoon at a time, until the dough is moistened. Form into a ball and refrigerate for 30 minutes.

Sauté the meat, garlic, and green onions in the oil until lightly browned, stirring from time to time. Add the soy sauce, sherry, curry powder, salt, and brown sugar to the meat mixture. Cook, stirring, for 5 minutes. Add the potato and egg to the meat mixture and combine thoroughly. Allow the mixture to cool.

Preheat the convection oven to 400 degrees for 5 to 10 minutes.

Roll the dough out on a lightly floured board and cut into 2-inch circles. Spoon approximately ½ teaspoon of filling into the center of each circle. Fold the dough over and seal the edges well.

Place the crescents on an unbuttered cookie sheet and convection-bake for 8 to 10 minutes, or until the crescents are lightly browned.

Yield: Approximately 48 crescents

SPICY BEEF IN A BLANKET

Appetizers in a crust seem to delight guests. This is a simple-to-prepare hors d'oeuvre that can be made in advance and either refrigerated or frozen. The cheese in the pastry creates an extra little surprise, as does the slightly spicy filling.

PASTRY

1⅓ cups all-purpose flour
½ teaspoon salt
4 tablespoons (½ stick) butter
¼ cup grated Cheddar cheese
3 to 4 tablespoons ice water

FILLING

1 pound ground beef
1 onion, peeled and chopped
1 clove garlic, peeled and mashed
½ cup breadcrumbs
1 teaspoon salt
¼ teaspoon freshly ground black pepper
2 tablespoons catsup
¼ teaspoon Tabasco or hot pepper sauce
2 eggs

Prepare the pastry first. In a small mixing bowl, combine the flour and salt. Cut the butter and cheese into the flour, using a pastry blender or two knives, until the particles are the size of small peas. Sprinkle ice water over the flour mixture, 1 tablespoon at a time, mixing with a fork until the dough is lightly moistened. Form the dough into a ball and refrigerate for 30 minutes.

Combine all the filling ingredients in a bowl and mix thoroughly. Form the mixture into 1-inch meat balls and set aside.

Roll the pastry dough out on a lightly floured board to a thickness of ⅛ inch, then cut into squares approximately 3 inches in size.

Place one beef ball in the center of each square of dough and seal the dough around the meat, making sure the meat is completely covered.

Place the beef balls on an unbuttered cookie sheet and convection-bake in a 400-degree oven for 20 to 30 minutes, or until the pastry is golden brown.

Yield: Approximately 24 beef balls

BAKED STUFFED MUSHROOMS

1 pound medium mushrooms
½ pound pork sausage meat
1 medium onion, peeled and chopped
½ cup breadcrumbs
2 tablespoons freshly grated Parmesan cheese
2 tablespoons light cream
2 tablespoons dry sherry or dry white wine

Clean the mushrooms and remove the stems. Chop the stems and reserve both stems and caps.

In a skillet, sauté the sausage meat until it begins to brown, then add the onion and chopped mushroom stems and continue to cook until the sausage meat is thoroughly cooked. Stir in the remaining ingredients.

Spoon the mixture into the mushroom caps, then place on an unbuttered cookie sheet and convection-bake in a 325-degree oven for 8 to 10 minutes.

Yield: Approximately 24 mushrooms

BAKED STUFFED CLAMS

18 cherrystone clams, shelled (one shell from each reserved), washed, and chopped
3 cloves garlic, peeled and mashed
2 tablespoons chopped fresh parsley
2 tablespoons lemon juice
2 tablespoons olive oil
½ cup clam juice
⅓ cup flavored breadcrumbs

Preheat the convection oven to Maximum temperature for 5 to 10 minutes.

Spoon the chopped clams into the reserved shells. Combine the garlic, parsley, lemon juice, olive oil, and clam juice and spoon over the clams. Sprinkle the clams with the breadcrumbs.

Convection-bake for 10 to 20 minutes, or until brown.

Yield: 18 stuffed clams

SPONGE ROLL WITH CHICKEN MORNAY

This recipe calls for an unsweetened sponge roll, which is first cousin to the jelly roll, and useful when you want to serve an interesting appetizer. Fill the sponge roll with curried chicken, top with sauce Mornay, and you have an elegant first course.

SPONGE ROLL

4 eggs, separated
¼ teaspoon cream of tartar
¼ teaspoon salt
⅓ cup all-purpose flour
¼ cup melted butter

CURRIED CHICKEN

2 hard-boiled eggs, chopped
2 cups chopped, cooked chicken
½ to 1 cup mayonnaise
2 green onions, or scallions, chopped
3 tablespoons chopped fresh parsley
1 teaspoon curry powder
Salt and freshly ground white pepper to taste

SAUCE MORNAY

2 tablespoons butter
1½ tablespoons all-purpose flour
1 cup milk, scalded
¼ teaspoon salt
¼ cup heavy sweet cream
⅓ cup grated Swiss cheese

Prepare the sponge roll first.

Preheat the convection oven to 350 degrees for 5 to 10 minutes. Butter a 15½ × 10½ × 1-inch jelly-roll pan. Line the bottom with waxed paper and butter again.

Beat the egg whites, cream of tartar, and salt until the egg whites are stiff but not dry.

In another bowl, beat the egg yolks until thick and lemon colored. Gradually incorporate the flour into the egg yolks. Gently fold the egg whites into the yolk-flour mixture and pour into the prepared pan.

Convection-bake for 18 to 20 minutes, or until the top of the sponge roll springs back when lightly touched with a finger. Loosen the sponge roll from the sides of the pan and invert onto a towel that has been covered with waxed paper. Gently pull the waxed paper off the bottom of the sponge roll. Carefully roll the sponge roll from one long side, jelly-roll fashion, along with the waxed paper on the towel. Wrap in the towel and allow to cool for 30 minutes.

Prepare the curried chicken by combining the eggs and chicken with ½ cup of the mayonnaise and all the other ingredients. Add mayonnaise to the desired consistency, and seasoning to taste, and reserve.

To prepare the sauce Mornay, melt the butter in a saucepan, add the flour, and cook, stirring, for 2 to 3 minutes. Off heat stir in the scalded milk and salt. Bring the sauce to a boil, stirring constantly. If the sauce has any lumps, beat with a wire whisk or egg beater. Reduce the heat and allow the sauce to simmer. Gradually stir in the cream, then gradually add the cheese. Cook only until the cheese is blended thoroughly with the rest of the sauce.

To assemble the roll, carefully unroll the sponge roll and brush with melted butter. Spread the filling over the roll and reroll. Gently reheat the sauce Mornay and spoon over the chicken-filled roll.

Slice and serve.

Serves: 6

HAM PUFFS

PUFF BATTER

1 cup water
¼ pound (1 stick) butter
1 cup all-purpose flour
¼ teaspoon salt
4 eggs, lightly beaten

FILLING

½ pound boiled ham, ground
1 medium onion, peeled and chopped
1 tablespoon chopped fresh parsley
½ teaspoon Dijon-type mustard
2 tablespoons mayonnaise
1 teaspoon pickle relish
¼ cup grated Swiss cheese

Preheat the convection oven to 325 degrees for 5 to 10 minutes. Butter a cookie sheet.

Prepare the batter first. In a small saucepan heat the water and butter to the boiling point. Stir in the flour and salt and continue stirring until the mixture leaves the side of the pan. Remove from the heat and stir in the eggs until the mixture is thoroughly combined.

Using a teaspoon, spoon the batter onto the buttered cookie sheet. Convection-bake for 15 to 20 minutes, or until the puffs are golden brown. Remove from the oven at once and slit the tops to allow steam to escape. Cool the puffs, then cut the tops off and set both tops and bottoms aside.

Combine all the ingredients for the filling, except for the cheese, and spoon into the puffs. Sprinkle the grated cheese on top and cover with the tops of the puffs.

The ham puffs may be refrigerated at this point. Before baking, however, allow them to return to room temperature.

Preheat the convection oven to 350 degrees for 5 to 10 minutes.

Place the puffs on a lightly greased cookie sheet and convection-bake for 10 minutes, or until thoroughly hot.

Yield: Approximately 24 miniature puffs

POTATO-CHEESE PUFFS

4 medium potatoes, peeled and cooked
2 tablespoons butter
½ cup grated Swiss cheese
½ cup grated sharp Cheddar cheese
¾ cup all-purpose flour
1 egg, lightly beaten
2 tablespoons mayonnaise
½ teaspoon salt
1 tablespoon grated onion
1 clove garlic, peeled and mashed

Preheat the convection oven to 400 degrees for 5 to 10 minutes. Butter a cookie sheet.

In a large mixing bowl, combine the potatoes with the butter and the cheeses. Mash and mix thoroughly, then stir in the remaining ingredients.

Fit a pastry tube with the star tip and fill with the mixture, then press out the puffs onto the well-buttered cookie sheet; or drop by heaping teaspoonfuls onto the cookie sheet.

Convection-bake for 15 to 20 minutes, or until lightly browned.

Yield: Approximately 30 puffs

3
ROASTING AND BROILING

ROAST AND BROILED DISHES

Roast Beef Dinner

Filet Mignon Bercy à la Gabriel

Filet of Beef Sabatini

Special Twice-Baked Potatoes with Caviar

Apricot-Glazed Beef

Meat Loaf Wellington

Stuffed Hamburgers

Bifteck Haché

Barbecued Fresh Ham

Sunday Dinner Fresh Ham

Ham Fiesta

Roast Leg of Lamb Chez Moi

Roast Rack of Lamb

Lamb Chops Family Style

Punjabi Lamb Spareribs

Roast Veal Shanks

Breast of Veal with Dilled Potato Stuffing

Veal Birds

Stuffed Roast Chicken Hungarian

California-Style Garlic Chicken

Honey Chicken

Chili Chicken

Birds in Cream

Caneton à l'Orange Claudie

Crispy Roast Duck

Tangy Duck Orientale

Apple-Stuffed Roast Goose

Roast Wild Duck

Roasts and broiled meats come out with a savory brown crust when cooked in a convection oven. Can meat cooked in a convection oven truly be called "broiled"? Well, meats *look* broiled—they're brown on top, moist within—but if you're faced with a purist asking that question, or if you're a purist yourself, call your hamburgers or steaks "convection broiled." By any name, they will be delicious.

GUIDE TO ROASTING

PREHEATING

To preheat or not to preheat was one of the questions when it came to testing the ovens and the recipes for this section of the book. Some manufacturers recommended preheating, others said it wasn't necessary. We found it was not necessary in most cases, and a help in the others. When adapting your own recipes, check with the manufacturer's directions and then do a little judicious experimenting.

FROZEN MEATS

Frozen meats can be roasted without thawing first. Obviously, it takes longer to cook frozen meats.

MEAT THERMOMETER

This is a most important tool when using a convection oven. Some ovens come with these thermometers, but don't despair if yours doesn't. Just buy the best thermometer you can find. Money should be no object at this time— accuracy is what counts.

TIMING

Cooling times will vary, depending on whether you're cooking a thick, chunky piece of meat or a thin, narrow one. Again, manufacturers have a range of timing suggestions, so you will have to do some testing when adapting your own recipes. The meat thermometer is a real source of help, and it's best to check meats 10 minutes before the end of the suggested cooking time. Remember, too, that meat continues to cook even after you take it out of the oven. This is important if you want a rare roast beef; however, pork should always be roasted until it is thoroughly well done.

TEMPERATURE

Once again, the temperatures recommended by manufacturers vary, and much depends on the meats being cooked. When adapting your own recipes, lower the given temperature for conventional roasting by 25 to 50 degrees, and then check with your handy, dandy oven thermometer as the meat roasts. Use the chart that came with your oven as a guide.

GUIDE TO BROILING

PREHEATING

Do preheat your convection oven to its maximum temperature when you're broiling.

FROZEN MEATS

Frozen meats can be broiled without thawing first, and once again, they will take longer than thawed meats.

TIMING

Timing depends on the thickness of the meat. Check the broiling chart that came with your oven, and use it as a guide.

FOR BEST RESULTS

Place the meat directly on the rack, so the hot air can reach all surfaces. Make sure that the meat is dry—it will brown better that way.

For darker browning, sprinkle paprika on a steak or chicken, brush chicken or fish with butter, and spread a bit of soy sauce or steak marinade on steak or chopped beef.

ROAST BEEF DINNER

There's nothing more delicious than a standing rib roast of beef. The convection oven turns out a roast that is particularly juicy and flavorful; however, you will have to do some experimenting with the time. Much depends on the size and shape of the roast, so check the meat with a meat thermometer or—if your oven has one—with a meat probe, to determine the proper degree of doneness.

While the meat roasts, potatoes and onions can cook at the same time in the oven. The fat rendering from the meat will flavor the potatoes, and with the addition of a green salad you will have a complete meal by the time the roast is cooked.

1 three-rib standing rib roast of beef
4 cloves garlic, peeled and cut into slivers
Salt, freshly ground black pepper, and paprika to taste
1 onion, peeled and thinly sliced
4 large potatoes, peeled and thinly sliced
½ cup beef broth

Pierce the fat on top of the roast beef and insert slivers of garlic into the meat. Score the fat, then season with salt, pepper, and paprika.

Place the rib roast directly on the rack over the drip pan and convection-roast in a 400-degree oven for 20 minutes. Reduce the heat to 325 degrees and place the onion and potato slices in the drip pan. Spoon the beef broth over the vegetables.

Roast the beef for 15 to 18 minutes a pound for rare, 19 to 24 minutes for medium, or 25 to 30 minutes for well done. Start timing from the moment you first put the meat in the oven, and check with a meat thermometer.

Serves: 6

FILET MIGNON BERCY À LA GABRIEL

4 individual filet mignon steaks, each
   approximately 1½ inches thick
Paprika and freshly ground black pepper
   to taste
¼ cup melted butter
6 shallots, peeled and chopped
¼ pound (1 stick) butter
1 cup dry white wine

Preheat the convection oven to Maximum for 10 to 15 minutes.

Sprinkle paprika and black pepper on the filets. Place the meat directly on the rack, and spoon 1 tablespoon of butter on each filet.

Place the rack directly over the drip pan and convection-broil the filets for 10 to 14 minutes for rare or 14 to 18 minutes for medium.

To prepare the Sauce Bercy, melt the ¼ pound butter in a saucepan. Sauté the shallots for 3 to 5 minutes, or until translucent. Add the wine to the saucepan, stir, and then cook the sauce over medium-high heat until it is reduced by half.

Place the broiled filets on a serving platter and pour the Sauce Bercy over. Serve with Special Twice-Baked Potatoes (page 31), which can be heated while the filets are cooking. Place a dollop of red salmon caviar on each potato and add a tomato and onion salad for the most elegant dinner possible.

Serves: 4

FILET OF BEEF SABATINI

3 tablespoons olive oil
2 pounds whole filet of beef
Salt and freshly ground black pepper to
   taste
1 onion, peeled and sliced
1 clove garlic, peeled and mashed
2 tomatoes, peeled and chopped
1 bay leaf
¼ teaspoon dried thyme
¼ cup brandy
1 cup beef broth

Heat the oil in a skillet and quickly brown the filet on all sides. Season the filet with salt and pepper and place in an ovenproof casserole.

Add all the other ingredients to the casserole, cover, and convection-roast in a 325-degree oven for 1 to 1¼ hours, or until the beef is tender.

Serves: 4 to 6

SPECIAL TWICE-BAKED POTATOES WITH CAVIAR

4 large baking potatoes
¼ pound (1 stick) melted butter
¼ cup heavy sweet cream
½ cup milk
Salt and freshly ground white pepper to
  taste
4 tablespoons red salmon caviar

Place the potatoes on rack and convection-bake in a 350-degree oven for 45 minutes, or until tender when pierced with a fork.

Carefully cut a slice off the top of each potato. Scoop the potato pulp from the shells, being careful not to break the potato skins, and spoon into a saucepan; reserve the shells.

Over low heat gradually add the butter, cream, and milk to the potatoes, mashing until the potatoes are free of lumps. (The potatoes can also be mashed in a food processor.) Season the mashed potatoes to taste, then pile back into the potato shells.

If serving with Filet Mignon Bercy (page 30), place the potatoes on a shallow ovenproof pan and convection-bake for 10 minutes in a Maximum oven while the filet cooks.

If serving with another entree, the potatoes may be heated in a 350-degree oven for 15 to 20 minutes, or until hot and crusty on top. Spoon 1 tablespoon of caviar on each potato before serving.

Serves: 4

APRICOT GLAZED BEEF

1 rump roast or second-cut brisket of
  beef (4 to 5 pounds)
2 cups beef broth
1 onion, peeled and sliced
2 cloves garlic, peeled and mashed
Salt and freshly ground black pepper to
  taste
1 cup apricot preserves
2 teaspoons lemon juice
Whole cloves

Place the meat in a 3-quart ovenproof casserole and add the broth, onion, garlic, and salt and pepper. Cover and convection-roast in a 350-degree oven for 2½ to 3 hours, or until the meat is tender.

In a bowl, combine the apricot preserves with the lemon juice. Mix thoroughly.

Uncover the meat, stud with cloves, and spread half of the apricot-lemon sauce over it. Continue cooking, uncovered, for 15 to 25 minutes, or until the meat is glazed.

Heat the remaining sauce and serve with the meat.

Serves: 8 to 10

MEAT LOAF WELLINGTON

Beef Wellington—a filet of beef baked in pastry—was turning up on so many menus that it was becoming boring, as well as expensive. Here's a more interesting, and less expensive, version of the same idea—meat loaf baked in a crust. This can make a Sunday family dinner something special, and it's most successful at a party when served buffet style.

MEAT LOAF

½ pound beef, ground
½ pound veal, ground
½ pound pork, ground
1½ cups breadcrumbs
2 eggs
1 medium onion, peeled and chopped
¼ cup light cream
10 mushrooms, minced
¼ cup dry white wine
1 teaspoon salt
½ teaspoon freshly ground black pepper

PASTRY

1⅓ cups all-purpose flour
½ teaspoon salt
¼ pound (1 stick) butter
3 to 4 tablespoons ice water

GLAZE

1 egg, beaten

In a large mixing bowl, combine all the meat loaf ingredients. Spoon the mixture into a well-buttered 8½ × 4½ × 2½-inch loaf pan, then convection-bake in a 350-degree oven for 45 minutes. Remove from the oven and allow to cool.

While the meat is cooling, prepare the pastry crust.

In a mixing bowl, combine the flour and salt. Cut the butter into flour, using a pastry blender or two knives, until the particles are the size of small peas. Sprinkle ice water over the dough, 1 tablespoon at a time, mixing with a fork until the dough is lightly moistened. Form into a ball and refrigerate for 30 minutes.

Roll out the dough into a 14 × 10-inch rectangle on a lightly floured board. Turn the cooled meat loaf carefully out of the pan and place in the center of the dough. Fold the ends over the meat, envelope style, being careful to seal well. Place, seam side down, on a floured cookie sheet. Brush beaten egg over the dough and decorate the top with scraps of dough cut into triangle or star shapes. Pierce the crust with a fork in two or three places, to allow steam to escape.

Convection-bake in a 350-degree oven for approximately 30 minutes, or until the pastry is brown.

Serves: 8

STUFFED HAMBURGERS

Convection ovens turn out the best hamburgers ever made. The meat is cooked directly on the rack, over the drip pan, and the hamburgers come out juicy and delicious. They're better prepared this way than in most microwave ovens, because they become brown and crusty on top, while remaining moist within.

Convection-broiled hamburgers are also juicier than those broiled in a regular oven or pan broiled on top of the stove. There are purists who maintain that convection-broiled hamburgers are not *broiled*—they're really roasted. Fine, call them "roast hamburgers" if you wish, but you'll also call them the best hamburgers you've ever tasted. Use your own favorite recipe, or try the one below for a more unusual flavor.

1 small onion, peeled and minced
4 tablespoons (½ stick) butter
1 pound chopped beef
Salt and freshly ground black pepper to taste

Preheat the convection oven to Maximum for 10 minutes.

Sauté the onion in the butter, stirring, until translucent but not brown.

Season the meat, then divide into 4 portions. Divide each portion in half and shape into a flat patty. Spoon one-fourth of the onion and butter mixture on the bottom half of each hamburger. Top with other half, then gently seal the edges of each onion-filled hamburger.

Put the hamburgers directly on the rack over the drip pan and convection-broil for 10 to 14 minutes for rare, or 12 to 17 minutes for medium. (These times are approximate. Check with the directions for your convection oven.)

Serves: 4

BIFTECK HACHÉ

This dish was developed when a sudden call to a friend's house turned four perfectly fine, broiled hamburgers into leftovers. A search in the refrigerator revealed a congealed dish of mashed potatoes—more leftovers. The two were combined with a few other ingredients and renamed *bifteck haché*, which is French for hamburgers.

"Delicious," was the verdict. "So glad we're not eating leftovers."

This recipe can easily be adapted to accommodate any interesting bits and pieces languishing in your refrigerator. Grind leftover cooked meat, add potatoes and seasonings, and your convection oven will quickly turn out a juicy casserole, with an appealing, crusty top.

1 pound ground beef, broiled
3 cups mashed potatoes
2 tablespoons catsup
1 onion, peeled and minced
1 green pepper, seeded and chopped
Salt and freshly ground black pepper to
    taste
6 tablespoons melted butter

Butter a 9-inch ovenproof casserole.

Mix all the ingredients thoroughly, spoon into the casserole, and convection-bake in a 350-degree oven for 20 to 30 minutes, or until the top is brown and crusty.

Serves: 4

BARBECUED FRESH HAM

1 fresh ham (5 to 6 pounds), rind
    removed
2 tablespoons vegetable oil
1 large onion, peeled and diced
2 cloves garlic, peeled and mashed
2 cups catsup
1 teaspoon Tabasco or hot pepper sauce
3 tablespoons Worcestershire sauce
1 teaspoon prepared mustard
½ cup firmly packed brown sugar
2 tablespoons wine vinegar
1 cup water

Score the fat and place the ham directly on the rack over the drip pan. Convection-roast in a 325-degree oven for 1¾ to 2 hours, or until the ham is thoroughly cooked and a meat thermometer registers 170 degrees. Baste the ham twice, during the last hour of cooking, with a barbecue sauce made the following way:

Heat the oil in a large skillet and sauté the onion and garlic until translucent. Add the remaining ingredients to the skillet and bring to a simmer, stirring until the sauce is thoroughly blended. Use the sauce for basting the ham, then heat the remainder and serve with the ham.

Serves: 6 to 8

SUNDAY DINNER FRESH HAM

1 fresh ham (5 to 6 pounds)
Salt and freshly ground black pepper
¼ cup vegetable oil
1 carrot, scraped and sliced
1 stalk celery, trimmed and sliced
1 large onion, peeled and sliced
3 cups chicken broth
½ cup dry white wine

If butcher has not done so, remove the rind from the ham. Score the fat and sprinkle the ham liberally with salt and pepper. Place the ham in either a double roasting pan or a Dutch oven, whichever container fits best in your convection oven.

Heat the oil in a large skillet and sauté the carrot, celery, and onion until the vegetables are translucent. Add the broth to the skillet and bring to a simmer. Pour the onion-broth sauce over the ham.

Cover the roaster or Dutch oven and convection-roast the ham in a 350-degree oven for 1¾ to 2 hours. Uncover and add the wine, then continue cooking for an additional hour, basting two or three times. The ham must be well done, and a meat thermometer should register 170 degrees.

Serves: 6 to 8

HAM FIESTA

1 cooked, cured ham (7 to 8 pounds)
2 onions, peeled and sliced
3 stalks celery, trimmed and sliced
4 sprigs parsley
1 bay leaf
½ cup dry white vermouth
2 cups chicken broth
¼ cup honey
¼ cup confectioners sugar

Preheat the convection oven to 350 degrees for 5 to 10 minutes.

Place the ham in a double roaster or large, ovenproof casserole. Add all the other ingredients, except for the honey and sugar, then cover and convection-roast for 1½ to 2 hours, basting occasionally. The ham is done when easily pierced by a fork.

Remove the ham from the casserole. Spread the honey on top and sprinkle with the sugar.

Raise the heat in the convection oven to 450 degrees.

Place the ham directly on the rack over the drip pan and cook for an additional 15 minutes, or until the top is brown and glazed.

Serves: 12 to 14

ROAST LEG OF LAMB CHEZ MOI

If you've always eaten leg of lamb well done, try it just once medium-rare and you may never go back to eating it the old way. Leg of lamb, prepared this way in a convection oven, has the wonderful flavor of lamb cooked outdoors over an open fire. Serve it with a tomato and onion salad, dressed with wine vinegar and olive oil.

1 leg of lamb (5 pounds)
2 cloves garlic, peeled and cut into slivers
Freshly ground black pepper and paprika to taste
¼ cup olive oil
1 onion, peeled and sliced
2 cups beef broth
½ cup dry white wine

Preheat the convection oven to 450 degrees for 5 to 10 minutes.

Make incisions all over the lamb and insert the garlic slivers. Season with pepper and paprika, then spread the olive oil over the lamb, using a spoon or spatula.

Place the onion slices in the drip pan. Put the lamb directly on the rack over the drip pan, add 1 cup of the broth to the drip pan, and convection-roast the lamb for 30 minutes. Baste the lamb with a combination of the remaining beef broth and wine and cook for an additional 40 to 50 minutes, or until a meat thermometer reads 140 degrees for medium-rare.

If you really do prefer your lamb well done, cook it for approximately 20 minutes longer, or until the meat thermometer reads 170 degrees.

Serve the lamb with the juices from the drip pan.

Serves: 6 to 8

ROAST RACK OF LAMB

Simple, and oh so delicious, is rack of lamb. This is an expensive dish, but well worth while on special occasions. Serve it with a watercress and endive salad and just a few butter-fried potatoes. If the butcher's bill makes you gasp, just comfort yourself with the thought that this easily prepared dish would cost twice as much in a restaurant.

1 rack of lamb consisting of 8 small rib chops; approximately 1½ pounds
Salt and freshly ground black pepper
1 cup water
2 tablespoons chopped fresh parsley

Preheat the convection oven to Maximum temperature.

Season the rack of lamb and score, then place the lamb directly on the rack over the drip pan. Add the cup of water to the drip pan.

Convection-broil for 15 to 25 minutes, or until a meat thermometer reads 140 to 150 degrees for medium-rare. Garnish with the parsley and present whole, with the pan juices, before slicing into individual chops.

Serves: 2

LAMB CHOPS FAMILY STYLE

4 shoulder lamb chops, each 1 inch thick
2 cloves garlic, peeled and mashed
Salt and freshly ground black pepper to taste
1 green pepper, seeded and cut into 4 rings
1 tomato, cut into 4 slices
¼ teaspoon dried oregano

Preheat the convection oven to Maximum temperature.

Spread the chops with garlic, season with salt and pepper, and place 1 green pepper ring and 1 slice of tomato on each chop. Sprinkle with the oregano.

Place the chops directly on the rack over the drip pan and convection-broil for 15 to 18 minutes for medium or 19 to 23 minutes for well done.

Serves: 4

PUNJABI LAMB SPARERIBS

Here's a simple version of lamb curry. To make it especially enticing, serve it with steamed rice and side dishes of chutney, unsweetened coconut shreds, peanuts, and a cucumber salad made by adding a chopped cucumber to a cup of plain yogurt and seasoning it with cumin, salt, and pepper.

4 pounds lamb spareribs, cut into 6 to 8 pieces
2 tablespoons vegetable oil
2 apples, cored and chopped
1 onion, peeled and sliced
1 clove garlic, peeled and mashed
¼ cup all-purpose flour
1 tablespoon curry powder
¼ teaspoon ground ginger
Salt and freshly ground black pepper to taste
2 cups chicken broth
1 tablespoon lemon juice
1 cup plain yogurt

Place the lamb spareribs directly on the rack over the drip pan and convection-roast in a 325-degree oven for 1 to 1½ hours, or until the meat is tender.

While the meat roasts, heat the oil in a large skillet and sauté the apple, onion, and garlic over low heat for 5 minutes, stirring. Add the flour, curry powder, ginger, and salt and pepper. Cook for 3 minutes, stirring.

Gradually add the chicken broth and lemon juice to the skillet. Cook over low heat, stirring constantly, until the sauce has thickened. Add the yogurt and heat thoroughly, without boiling, before pouring over the cooked meat.

Serves: 6

ROAST VEAL SHANKS

2 tablespoons olive oil
2 tablespoons butter
4 veal shanks
Salt and freshly ground black pepper to taste
1 onion, diced
2 stalks celery, trimmed and sliced
1 cup chicken broth
½ cup dry sherry

Heat the oil and butter in a large skillet and brown the veal shanks on all sides, then place in a 3-quart ovenproof casserole. Season with salt and pepper and set aside.

Sauté the onion and celery in the skillet until translucent. Add the chicken broth to the skillet and bring to a simmer. Off heat, stir in the sherry, then pour the contents of the skillet over the veal shanks.

Cover and convection-roast in a 350-degree oven for 1¾ to 2 hours, or until the meat is tender. Serve with buttered noodles.

Serves: 4

BREAST OF VEAL WITH DILLED POTATO STUFFING

1 breast of veal (4 to 4½ pounds), with
  a pocket for stuffing
1 clove garlic, peeled and cut into slivers
Salt, freshly ground black pepper, and
  paprika to taste
2 potatoes, peeled, cooked, and mashed
2 tablespoons chopped fresh dill
4 tablespoons (½ stick) butter, softened
2 cups chicken broth
1 tomato, peeled and chopped
½ cup dry white wine

Cut small incisions in the veal and insert the garlic slivers. Season the veal liberally with salt, pepper, and paprika.

Combine the mashed potatoes with the chopped dill and salt, mixing well. Stuff the veal with the potato mixture, closing the pocket with small metal skewers.

Place the veal in a 3-quart ovenproof baking dish and spread with the softened butter. Add the chicken broth and tomato to the casserole, cover, and convection-roast in a 350-degree oven for 1 hour.

Uncover the veal, add the wine, and cook for an additional 1 to 1½ hours, or until the veal is brown and tender. Baste occasionally while the veal is uncovered.

Serves: 4

VEAL BIRDS

4 veal cutlets, pounded thin
4 thin slices boiled ham
¼ cup freshly grated Parmesan cheese
Freshly ground black pepper to taste
4 slices bacon
3 teaspoons dried thyme
Salt to taste
4 tablespoons (½ stick) melted butter

Place a slice of ham on each piece of veal and sprinkle with the cheese and black pepper. Roll up each piece of veal and wrap a slice of bacon around each roll. Secure with a metal skewer.

Sprinkle each veal bird with thyme and salt, then spoon the melted butter into a shallow, ovenproof dish and place the veal birds in the dish.

Convection-roast in a 350-degree oven for 20 to 30 minutes, turning once.

Serves: 2

STUFFED ROAST CHICKEN HUNGARIAN

Hungarian cooks traditionally stuff chickens, and other birds for roasting, between the skin and the breast meat of the birds. This requires careful handling—it's important not to tear the skin when loosening it from the meat—but the result is worth the care. The bird looks especially plump, because as the stuffing cooks it tends to puff up. In addition, the breast meat is never dry and the bird is exceptionally succulent.

1 chicken (2½ to 3 pounds)
4 tablespoons (½ stick) butter
1 medium onion, peeled and chopped
3 apples, peeled, cored, and chopped
2 cups breadcrumbs
1 teaspoon salt
¼ teaspoon freshly ground black pepper
½ teaspoon poultry seasoning
1 cup chicken broth

Wash the chicken and pat dry. Set aside.

Melt the butter in a medium-sized skillet. Sauté the onion and apple until lightly browned. Add the breadcrumbs, seasoning, and broth and mix until thoroughly combined. Allow the stuffing to cool.

Loosen the skin from the breast and leg area of the chicken, being very careful not to tear the skin. Gently push the stuffing under the skin. If there is any stuffing left over, spoon it into the chicken cavity.

Place the chicken on the rack above the drip pan and convection-roast in a 325-degree oven for 1 hour and 10 minutes to 1 hour and 20 minutes, or until the chicken is nicely browned and the meat thermometer reads 185 degrees.

Serves: 4

Variation:
Prepare a bread stuffing with 2 cups bread crumbs, ¼ cup butter, 1 clove garlic peeled and mashed, ¼ cup chopped fresh parsley, 1 beaten egg, salt, freshly ground black pepper, and paprika to taste.

CALIFORNIA-STYLE GARLIC CHICKEN

Five cloves of garlic may sound like a lot for one chicken, but much of the garlic pungency evaporates as the garlic cooks. There is enough left to flavor the chicken deliciously, especially when combined with the other ingredients in the following marinade.

5 cloves garlic, peeled and mashed
1 tablespoon lemon juice
2 tablespoons butter
1 tablespoon olive oil
½ cup dry white wine
1 bay leaf
½ teaspoon salt
1 teaspoon Dijon-type mustard
½ cup chicken broth
1 tablespoon chopped fresh parsley
1 chicken (2½ to 3 pounds), cut into eight pieces

Combine all the ingredients except for the chicken. Place the chicken in a shallow dish and pour the marinade mixture over. Allow to marinate for 1 hour, turning the chicken every 15 to 20 minutes.

Preheat the convection oven to Maximum for 10 minutes.

Place the chicken on the rack over the drip pan and spoon the marinade over. Convection-broil for 25 to 30 minutes.

Serve with the sauce from the drip pan.

Serves: 4

HONEY CHICKEN

1 chicken (3 to 3½ pounds), cut into eight pieces
1 fresh hot chili pepper, seeded and minced (optional)
¼ cup soy sauce
2 tablespoons catsup
½ cup vinegar
¼ cup honey
¼ cup water

Preheat the convection oven to Maximum temperature.

Place the chicken directly on the rack over the drip pan. Convection-broil for 30 to 40 minutes, or until the chicken is brown and crispy.

While the chicken is broiling, combine all the other ingredients in a saucepan and simmer for 5 to 10 minutes over low heat, stirring occasionally.

After the chicken has broiled for 25 minutes, baste it with the sauce, and 10 minutes later baste once again. Pour any remaining sauce over the cooked chicken before serving.

Serves: 4

CHILI CHICKEN

3 cloves garlic, peeled and mashed
2 teaspoons chili powder
1 cup plain yogurt
1 chicken (2½ to 3 pounds), cut into eight pieces

Combine the garlic, chili powder, and yogurt. Mix well, pour over the chicken, and marinate overnight.

Preheat the convection oven to Maximum for 5 to 10 minutes.

Place the chicken directly on the rack over the drip pan. Convection-broil for 25 to 35 minutes, or until the chicken is brown and tender.

Serves: 4

BIRDS IN CREAM

This recipe calls for Rock Cornish game hens, but should they be unavailable the dish can be successfully prepared with small broilers that have been split in two. The wine and cream sauce give this dish an air of luxury, but the ingredients are far from expensive.

2 Rock Cornish game hens (approximately 1 to 1½ pounds each), split
Salt and freshly ground white pepper to taste
¼ teaspoon *herbes de Provence* or ⅛ teaspoon dried thyme and 1 bay leaf, crushed
Paprika
¼ pound (1 stick) butter
½ cup dry white vermouth
1 cup heavy sweet cream

Preheat the convection oven to Maximum temperature.

Season the birds with salt and pepper. Crush the *herbes de Provence*, or thyme and bay leaf, and sprinkle in the birds' cavities. Sprinkle paprika on all sides.

Place the birds directly on the oven rack over the drip pan and dot with butter. Convection-broil for 20 to 25 minutes, or until the birds are brown and crisp.

Turn the convection oven off and allow the birds to remain in the turned-off oven. Remove the pan and pour the pan juices into a skillet. Add the vermouth and cook for 5 minutes, until the juices are syrupy. Over low heat, gradually stir in the cream. Simmer for 5 minutes, stirring.

Correct the seasoning, pour the sauce over the birds, and serve.

Serves: 4

CANETON À L'ORANGE CLAUDIE

French ducklings are different from the ducklings available in the United States. The French birds are elegantly lean, without the fat under the skin that's found in American-bred birds. A famous chef who oversees the kitchens of one of New York's finest restaurants said that convection-oven roasting is the perfect way to prepare American ducklings. The fat renders, and the duckling becomes delectably crisp.

Here is a recipe for French orange duckling adapted to the convection oven. This version of the orange sauce was created in Paris by Madame Claudie, and is named for her.

1 duckling (4 to 5 pounds), giblets reserved
Salt
1 carrot, scraped and sliced
1 onion, peeled and sliced
1 clove garlic, peeled
¼ teaspoon dried thyme
1 cup water
2 cups dry white wine
2 tablespoons granulated sugar
1 tablespoon wine vinegar
Juice of 2 oranges
2 tablespoons cornstarch
2 tablespoons currant jelly
¼ cup Grand Marnier
1 orange, halved and thinly sliced

Sprinkle the duck lightly both inside and out with salt, then set aside.

Place the duck giblets, carrot, onion, and garlic in a shallow ovenproof pan. Sprinkle with the thyme, then convection-roast in a 325-degree oven for 15 minutes. Remove from the oven and reserve.

Prick the duck skin with a sharp knife, especially on the breast and around the drumsticks. Place the duck directly on the rack over the drip pan and convection-roast in a 400-degree oven for 1 hour.

While the duck is roasting, prepare the orange sauce.

Place the giblets and vegetables in a large saucepan. Add the water and wine, then cover and simmer for 30 minutes.

Melt the sugar in a heavy saucepan, and as it begins to caramelize, add the vinegar and orange juice. Bring to a simmer, stirring to dissolve the caramel, and cook for 2 to 3 minutes.

Strain the stock from the giblets. Combine ½ cup of the stock with the cornstarch. Mix well, then add to the sauce, along with the remaining stock. Add the currant jelly and allow the sauce to simmer for 3 to 5 minutes, or until the sauce has thickened and is clear. Off heat, stir in the Grand Marnier.

Brush the sauce over the duck and continue roasting for an additional 30 to 40 minutes, or until the meat thermometer registers 180 to 185 degrees.

Add the orange slices to the sauce and heat thoroughly over a low flame.

Before serving, carve the duck and pour the sauce over all.

Serves: 4

CRISPY ROAST DUCK

1 tablespoon salt
3 cloves garlic, peeled and mashed
2 teaspoons paprika
1 duckling (5 to 6 pounds)

Combine the salt, garlic, and paprika and spread the mixture liberally on the duck. Sprinkle the remainder of the mixture in the cavity of the duck.

Prick the duck skin with a sharp knife, especially on the breast and around the drumsticks, to permit the fat to render. Place duck directly on the rack over the drip pan and convection-roast in a 400-degree oven for 1½ to 1¾ hours, or until a meat thermometer reads 180 to 185 degrees.

If a great deal of fat accumulates, pour it off from the drip pan from time to time.

The duck should be very tender and crispy when cooked.

Serves: 4

TANGY DUCK ORIENTALE

1 cup firmly packed dark brown sugar
1 tablespoon ground cinnamon
2 whole cloves
½ cup water
1 tablespoon soy sauce
1 teaspoon ground ginger
1 duckling (4 to 5 pounds)
3 cups sauerkraut, drained
½ cup pineapple juice

Combine the sugar, cinnamon, cloves, and water in a saucepan. Cook over low heat, stirring, until the sugar melts. Continue cooking until a syrup is formed. Stir in the soy sauce and ginger, remove from the heat, and set aside.

With a small sharp knife, prick the duckling all over, especially in the fatty areas over breast and drumsticks. This will permit fat to render.

Place the duck directly on the rack over the drip pan and convection-roast in a 400-degree oven for 1 hour and 10 minutes.

Brush the sauce over the duck and continue roasting for an additional 20 to 30 minutes, or until a meat thermometer reads 180 to 185 degrees.

While the duck is roasting, combine the remainder of the sauce with the sauerkraut and pineapple juice. Pour into an ovenproof casserole, then cover and convection-cook for the last 15 minutes of the duck's roasting time.

Place the duck on a platter. Spoon the sauerkraut mixture around the duck and serve.

Serves: 4

APPLE-STUFFED ROAST GOOSE

¼ pound (1 stick) butter, more if desired
2 onions, peeled and chopped
1 garlic clove, peeled and mashed
10 apples, peeled, cored, and chopped
2 tablespoons chopped fresh parsley
1 egg, lightly beaten
3 cups breadcrumbs or bread stuffing
1 goose (8 to 10 pounds)
Salt and freshly ground black pepper to
  taste

Melt the butter in a large skillet and sauté the onion and garlic until translucent. Add the chopped apple to the skillet and continue cooking until the apple breaks up easily with a fork. Add the parsley, egg, and breadcrumbs or bread stuffing. Cook the stuffing over a low flame, combining thoroughly and adding more butter if a moister stuffing is desired. Season to taste and allow the stuffing to cool.

Season the goose with salt and pepper. Fill the cavity with the stuffing and secure the opening with metal skewers.

Place the goose directly on the rack over the drip pan and convection-roast in a 400-degree oven for 45 minutes. Drain the accumulated fat from the drip pan and save (goose fat can be used in cassoulet, or for frying potatoes).

Lower the oven temperature to 325 degrees and continue to roast for 1¼ to 1½ hours, or until a meat thermometer placed in the thigh reads 180 to 185 degrees. If the thermometer is not used, press the meaty part of a leg between protected fingers; it should feel tender. Test also by pricking the leg with a fork; the juices should be tan, not red.

Serves: 6 to 9

ROAST WILD DUCK

Convection roasting is a fine way to prepare game fowl. The juices are sealed in, and the meat does not dry out. Interesting dishes to serve with roast wild duck are braised celery, a puree of white beans and chestnuts, or baked sweet potatoes. An endive and watercress salad is also a fine accompaniment.

1 wild duck (about 2 to 2½ pounds)
Paprika
4 slices bacon
2 tablespoons butter

Sprinkle the duck liberally with paprika both inside and out. Place the bacon slices across the breast of the duck and put the butter in the cavity.

Place the duck directly on the rack over the drip pan and convection-roast in a 400-degree oven for 45 to 55 minutes, or until a meat thermometer reads 180 to 185 degrees.

Serves: 2

4
FISH AND SHELLFISH

FISH AND SHELLFISH

Baked Bluefish or Striped Bass

Salmon Steaks with Cucumber Cream

Swordfish Kebabs with Lime

Breaded Fish Fillets

Baked Shad in Cream

Creole Casserole

Spicy Shrimp Marbella

Herb McCarthy's Bowden Square Lobster

Can you use a convection oven to cook fish and shellfish? Yes, very successfully. There is far less chance of the fish becoming a dry piece of cardboard when you use a convection oven; fish dishes come out moist and delicious. Flavors are sealed in, as the fish cooks at a lower temperature in a shorter time.

There's another plus: thanks to the constantly circulating air, you can cook fish while you cook other dishes. Fish odors will not cling to rice, rolls, or vegetables.

The following chart for convection-cooking fish should be used as a guide when adapting your favorite recipes. The times are approximate, because much depends on the size and thickness of the fish.

When using frozen fish, thaw before convection cooking.

WHEN YOU CONVECTION-COOK FISH

Type of Fish	Temperature	Time
Dressed, or whole, large fish	300 degrees	45 to 60 minutes
Pan-dressed, or smaller, whole fish	300 degrees	25 to 30 minutes
Fillets, fresh or frozen and thawed	300 to 350 degrees	15 to 20 minutes
Steaks	Maximum or broil	15 to 18 minutes
Steaks baked with sauce	350 degrees	25 to 30 minutes

BAKED BLUEFISH OR STRIPED BASS

6 tablespoons melted butter
1 bluefish or striped bass (2 to 2½ pounds), split
Salt and freshly ground black pepper to taste
4 sprigs fresh dill
Juice of ½ lemon
Paprika
½ cup dry white wine
1 lemon, sliced
4 tablespoons chopped parsley

Spoon half of the melted butter into the fish's cavity. Sprinkle liberally with salt and pepper and add the dill weed and lemon juice.

Place the fish in a shallow ovenproof dish. Pour the remaining butter on top, then sprinkle liberally with paprika. Pour the white wine into the dish and convection-bake in a 300-degree oven for 25 to 30 minutes, or until the fish flakes easily with a fork.

Garnish the fish with lemon slices and parsley and serve immediately.

Serves: 4 to 6

SALMON STEAKS WITH CUCUMBER CREAM

2 tablespoons butter
4 individual salmon steaks
Salt and freshly ground black pepper
4 tablespoons lemon juice
1 small cucumber, peeled and chopped
2 tablespoons chopped fresh dill
2 cups sour cream

Butter an ovenproof baking dish.

Season the salmon steaks on both sides with salt and pepper, then place in the baking dish. Spoon 1 tablespoon of lemon juice over each steak.

Combine the cucumber, dill, and sour cream and spoon over the salmon, then convection-bake in a 350-degree oven for 25 to 30 minutes, or until the salmon flakes easily with a fork.

Serves: 4

SWORDFISH KEBABS WITH LIME

½ cup fresh lime juice
½ cup olive oil
½ teaspoon dried thyme
2 pounds swordfish, cut into large cubes
2 limes, cut into rounds
Salt and freshly ground black pepper to taste

Combime the lime juice, olive oil, and thyme and marinate the fish in this combination for 2 hours.

Preheat the convection oven to Maximum for 10 minutes. Butter a shallow ovenproof pan.

Thread the fish cubes and lime rounds on skewers, and season. Place the skewers on the buttered pan and convection-broil for 10 to 15 minutes, or until the fish flakes easily with a fork.

Pour the remainder of the marinade over fish and serve.

Serves: 4

BREADED FISH FILLETS

Many people love fried fish, but they don't love the extra calories that come with it. Here's a recipe for breaded fish fillets, baked in a convection oven. Simple—no need to turn or baste—and every bit as crispy as fried fish, but minus calories and cholesterol.

4 fish fillets, fresh or frozen and thawed
Salt and freshly ground white pepper
½ cup milk
2 cups breadcrumbs
4 tablespoons melted butter
4 lemon wedges
4 tablespoons chopped parsley

Season the fish, then dip each fillet in milk. Roll the fillets in the breadcrumbs.

Place the fish directly on the rack over the drip pan. Spoon the butter over the fish and convection-bake in a 350-degree oven for 15 to 20 minutes, or until the fillets are brown and flake easily when tested with a fork.

Garnish with lemon wedges and parsley and serve immediately.

Serves: 4

BAKED SHAD IN CREAM

1 shad (3 pounds), boned and split
Salt, freshly ground black pepper, and
    paprika to taste
4 tablespoons melted butter
1 cup heavy sweet cream

Butter an ovenproof dish and place the shad in it. Sprinkle with salt, pepper, and paprika and pour the melted butter over. Convection-bake in a 300-degree oven for 15 to 20 minutes.

Pour the cream over the shad and bake for another 10 to 15 minutes, or until the fish flakes easily with a fork.

Serves: 6

CREOLE CASSEROLE

6 slices bacon
1 small onion, peeled and chopped
1 clove garlic, peeled and mashed
1 green pepper, seeded and chopped
2 stalks celery, trimmed and chopped
2 cups cubed, cooked chicken
½ pound boiled shrimp, each shrimp
    peeled and cut in half
1 cup raw rice
2 cups chicken broth
¼ teaspoon ground cumin
2 cups cooked fresh or canned plum
    tomatoes, chopped
Salt and freshly ground black pepper to
    taste

Fry the bacon in a large skillet. Remove the cooked bacon and reserve, then sauté the onion, garlic, pepper, and celery in the bacon grease until translucent.

Add the chicken and shrimp, and cook, stirring, an additional 3 minutes, then add all the other ingredients to the skillet and cook, stirring, for 3 minutes more, until the mixture is thoroughly combined.

Spoon the contents of the skillet into an ovenproof casserole. Top with the reserved bacon, cover, and convection-bake in a 350-degree oven for 45 to 50 minutes, or until the rice is cooked.

Serves: 4

SPICY SHRIMP MARBELLA

6 tablespoons olive oil
3 cloves garlic, peeled and mashed
½ fresh hot chili pepper, seeded and
   minced
1 pound raw shrimp, peeled and
   deveined

Preheat the convection oven to Maximum temperature for 5 to 10 minutes.

Heat the oil in a skillet and add the garlic and hot chili pepper. Cook, stirring, for 2 to 3 minutes.

Place the shrimp in an ovenproof casserole and spoon the garlic-pepper mixture over. Convection-broil for 8 to 10 minutes, depending on the size of the shrimp.

Serve over rice.

Serves: 2

HERB McCARTHY'S BOWDEN SQUARE LOBSTER

Herb McCarthy's Bowden Square restaurant in Southampton is famous far beyond the South Shore of Long Island for its succulent lobster. Many people drive for a hundred miles—from New York City—or even further for one of Herb's broiled lobsters. When asked how he managed to serve a broiled lobster that was always delicious, never dry, Herb led us into his kitchen, and showed us—you guessed it—his convection oven. Here is Herb's recipe for convection-broiled lobster.

2 lobsters (1½ to 1¾ pounds), each split
   and stomach sac removed from head
5 tablespoons melted butter, plus extra
   for serving
2 tablespoons breadcrumbs
3 tablespoons dry white wine
Paprika
Lemon wedges

Preheat the convection oven to 375 degrees for 20 minutes.

Make a paste of the 5 tablespoons butter, the breadcrumbs, and white wine. Spread on the lobster meat and sprinkle paprika on top.

Place the lobsters directly on the rack over the drip pan and convection-broil for 20 to 22 minutes, depending on the size of the lobster.

Serve with extra melted butter and lemon wedges. And with the lobsters Herb recommends a dry white wine, such as a California Sauvignon Blanc.

Serves: 2

5
CASSEROLES, STEWS, AND A POTAGE

CASSEROLES, STEWS, AND A POTAGE

Beef 'n' Rice Hotpot

Down Home Beef 'n' Vegetable Stew

Gingery Sauerbraten

Pumpkin Surprise

Herbed Brisket of Beef

Bavarian Beef Rolls

Carbonnades à la Flamande

The Caliph's Lamb

Moussaka

Country Kitchen Lamb 'n' Biscuits

Lamb Shanks Italian

Cassoulet

Glazed Pineapple Pork Chops

Fireside Pork and Apple Casserole

Potato and Pork Casserole

Cantonese Pork with Stir-Fried Vegetables

Sausage Bake

Tuscan Veal Chops with Mushrooms

Chicken Basquaise

Chicken and Rice Paprika

Morning-After Onion Soup with Béchamel Sauce

Potage Basquaise

Casseroles do not cook as quickly in a convection oven as roasts do, because the casserole dish prevents the circulating air from reaching all surfaces at the same time.

However, cooking time *is* reduced, and there's no need to preheat the convection oven to cook the casserole.

Whenever possible, choose a shallow casserole over a deep one. No need to buy special equipment, though—any ovenproof dish that fits into your convection oven can be used.

Most casseroles are cooked with a cover at least part of the time, because the intensity of convection heat can cause the top of a casserole to dry out.

An imaginative casserole, baked in a convection oven, can be brought proudly to the dinner table whether for a family group or to please a special gathering of friends. Casseroles really call for a great deal more creativity than a simple—albeit expensive—roast, and they're rewarding to the cook because of the delicious flavor as well as the money saved.

BEEF 'N' RICE HOTPOT

2 onions, peeled and diced
¼ cup vegetable oil
1 clove garlic, peeled and mashed
1 pound ground beef
2 cups stewed tomatoes, chopped
½ cup raw rice
2 teaspoons chili powder
Salt and freshly ground black pepper to
    taste

In a large skillet, sauté the onions in the oil until translucent. Add the garlic and cook an additional 2 minutes. Add the beef and cook until the meat has lost its raw, red look. Add all the other ingredients, combining thoroughly.

Spoon the mixture into a lightly greased 2-quart ovenproof casserole. Cover and convection-bake in a 350-degree oven for 35 to 40 minutes, then uncover and bake an additional 15 minutes.

Serves: 4 to 6

DOWN HOME BEEF 'N' VEGETABLE STEW

2 pounds boneless stewing beef, cut into
    1-inch cubes
Salt and freshly ground black pepper to
    taste
1 cup all-purpose flour
6 tablespoons vegetable oil
3 onions, peeled and diced
2 carrots, scraped and sliced
2 stalks celery, trimmed and sliced
4 large potatoes, peeled and cubed
½ teaspoon caraway seeds
2 cups tomato sauce
3 cups beef broth
1 package (10 ounces) frozen green peas
1 package (10 ounces) frozen cut string
    beans

Season the beef liberally with salt and pepper, then roll in the flour. Heat the vegetable oil in a large skillet and brown the meat on all sides. Remove the meat to a 3-quart ovenproof casserole.

In the same skillet, sauté the onions, carrots, and celery. Cook, stirring, for 5 minutes, then add to the meat. Add the potatoes, caraway seeds, tomato sauce, and beef broth to the casserole. Cover and convection-cook in a 325-degree oven for 1 hour.

Add the peas and string beans to the casserole and cook, covered, for an additional 30 minutes, or until the meat, potatoes, and vegetables are tender.

Serves: 4

GINGERY SAUERBRATEN

1 chuck roast (4 pounds)
1 teaspoon salt
½ teaspoon freshly ground black pepper
2 cups water
2 cups cider vinegar
1 cup dry red wine
1 onion, peeled and chopped
2 bay leaves
6 whole cloves
1 cup chopped celery leaves
¼ teaspoon dried thyme
¼ cup granulated sugar
All-purpose flour
¼ cup vegetable oil
½ cup dark raisins
12 gingersnaps, crushed

Season the beef with salt and pepper and place in a large bowl.

In a large saucepan, combine all the other ingredients except for the flour, oil, raisins, and gingersnaps. Bring to a boil and pour over the meat, then cover and refrigerate overnight.

Remove the meat from the marinade and dry with paper towels; reserve the marinade. Dredge the meat in flour and brown in hot oil in a large skillet.

Place the meat in a 3-quart ovenproof casserole and add 3 cups of the marinade. Cover and convection-cook in a 350-degree oven for 2¼ to 2¾ hours, or until the meat is tender.

Remove the meat and add the raisins and gingersnaps to the sauce. Stir the sauce and place the meat in the casserole once again. Cover and convection-cook an additional 15 minutes, or until the sauce is hot and thickened.

Slice the meat and pour the sauce over to serve.

Serves: 6 to 8

PUMPKIN SURPRISE

Imagine bringing a whole baked pumpkin to your dining table, lifting off the top, and serving a spicy beef stew that has been simmering within. That's what Pumpkin Surprise is all about. To prepare this dish, you must first find a well-shaped, unblemished pumpkin, of approximately 4 pounds. Be careful not to buy a pumpkin that's too large for your convection oven.

Your family and guests will enjoy this dish and the unique way it's presented. Cinderella's fairy godmother could turn a pumpkin into a coach, and now you can convert a pumpkin into a tureen.

2 pounds boneless rump or shoulder of beef cut into 2-inch cubes
¼ cup olive oil
1 onion, peeled and chopped
2 tomatoes, peeled, seeded, and chopped
2 apples, peeled and sliced
6 purple plums (fresh or canned), halved and pitted
3 tablespoons white raisins
1 lemon, cut into rounds
¼ teaspoon ground cumin
Salt and freshly ground black pepper to taste
1 medium pumpkin (approximately 4 pounds), round in shape
3 tablespoons butter, softened

In a large ovenproof skillet with a cover, sauté the beef in the olive oil until brown.

Add the onion, tomatoes, fruit, raisins, the lemon slices, cumin, and salt and pepper to the skillet, stirring to combine. Cover and convection-cook in a 325-degree oven for 30 minutes.

Meanwhile, using a sharp knife, cut a cover from the top of the pumpkin. Don't cut too far down or the pumpkin-tureen won't be deep enough. Scrape out the seeds and stringy material from inside the pumpkin and its cover. If the hollow does not seem large enough to accommodate the meat, scoop out some of the pumpkin flesh as well. Spread the softened butter on the inside of the pumpkin and sprinkle lightly with salt.

Spoon the contents of the skillet into the pumpkin. Cover with the pumpkin top and convection-bake in a 325-degree oven for 1 to 1½ hours, or until the pumpkin is tender. Do not overcook; the pumpkin must retain its shape and not collapse when you bring it to the table.

Serve by spooning beef and scooped-out pieces of pumpkin onto individual plates.

Serves: 6

HERBED BRISKET OF BEEF

1 brisket of beef (thick or second cut) or rump roast (4 to 5 pounds)
3 cloves garlic, peeled and cut into slivers
1 teaspoon paprika
3 tablespoons olive oil
2 medium onions, peeled and sliced
¼ cup chopped fresh dill
2 cups stewed tomatoes, chopped
2 cups beef broth
¼ cup chopped fresh parsley
Salt and freshly ground black pepper to taste

Wipe the brisket, then dry with paper towels. Make small gashes in the brisket and insert the garlic slivers in meat. Sprinkle the meat with the paprika.

Heat the oil in a large skillet. When the oil is hot, brown the meat on all sides over medium-low heat. After the meat has browned, place in a 4-quart oven-proof casserole.

Sauté the onions in the skillet until lightly browned, then add to the meat. Add half of the chopped dill and all the other ingredients to the casserole. Cover and convection-cook in a 350-degree oven for 2½ to 3 hours.

Add the remaining dill and serve.

Serves: 6 to 8

BAVARIAN BEEF ROLLS

1 pound boneless top round of beef, cut into 4 slices, each approximately 3 × 6 × ½ inches
¼ cup Dijon-type mustard
½ pound pork, ground
4 strips carrots
4 strips sweet pickle
Salt and freshly ground black pepper to taste
1 carrot, scraped and sliced
1 onion, peeled and sliced
1 clove garlic, peeled and mashed
4 cups beef broth
3 tablespoons butter
2 tablespoons all-purpose flour

Coat each beef slice with mustard. Divide the ground pork into four portions and place one portion on each beef slice. Top with a carrot and pickle strip and season with salt and pepper.

Roll each beef slice and tie with butcher's twine.

Place the carrot and onion slices and the garlic in the bottom of a 2-quart ovenproof casserole. Place the beef rolls on top, add 1 cup of the beef broth, and convection-cook in a 350-degree oven for 20 to 30 minutes, or until the beef rolls are brown. Add the remaining beef broth to the pan, cover, and continue cooking for an additional 1 to 1½ hours, or until the beef is fork tender.

Melt the butter in a saucepan. Add the flour and cook, stirring, until the roux is a light brown color.

Remove the beef rolls from the casserole. Stir the roux into the casserole, blending thoroughly. Return the beef rolls to the casserole and continue to cook, uncovered, for 15 minutes, or until the sauce is thick and both the beef and sauce are hot.

Serves: 4

CARBONNADES À LA FLAMANDE

3 tablespoons vegetable oil
4 pounds beef, from the rump, cut into strips approximately 2 × 4 × ½ inches
4 large onions, peeled and sliced
3 cloves garlic, peeled and mashed
1 cup beef broth
2 cups light beer
4 tablespoons brown sugar
5 sprigs parsley
1 teaspoon dried thyme
1 bay leaf
Salt and freshly ground black pepper to taste
2 tablespoons wine vinegar
1½ tablespoons cornstarch

Heat the oil in a large skillet and brown the beef slices.

Remove the beef to a 3-quart ovenproof casserole and sauté the onions in the skillet for about 10 minutes, or until the onion slices are translucent. Add the garlic and sauté for another minute, stirring. Add the onions and garlic to the casserole.

Combine the beef broth, beer, and brown sugar and stir well. Pour over the meat. Add the parsley, thyme, and bay leaf, then season to taste. Cover the casserole and convection-cook in a 325-degree oven for 1¼ to 1½ hours, or until the meat is tender.

Combine the vinegar and cornstarch in a small bowl, mixing well. Add the vinegar-cornstarch mixture to the casserole, then cook, uncovered, for 15 minutes, or until the sauce has thickened.

Correct the seasoning and serve.

Serves: 6 to 8

THE CALIPH'S LAMB

¼ cup olive oil
2 pounds lean, boneless stewing lamb, cut into 2-inch cubes
¼ cup all-purpose flour
1 onion, peeled and minced
½ teaspoon saffron, dissolved in 2 tablespoons water
½ teaspoon ground cinnamon
1 cup halved, pitted dates
10 dried apricots, cut in half
1 cup raw rice
2½ cups chicken broth
Salt and freshly ground black pepper to taste

Heat the olive oil in a large skillet. Toss the lamb in the flour, shaking off excess, and sauté quickly in the oil until brown. Remove the lamb to a 2-quart ovenproof casserole.

Add the onion to the skillet and cook, stirring from time to time, for 5 minutes, then add, along with all the other ingredients except the salt and pepper, to the casserole. Stir and cover.

Convection-bake in a 350-degree oven for 45 minutes to 1 hour, or until the liquid is absorbed and the lamb is tender.

Season to taste and serve.

Serves: 4 to 6

MOUSSAKA

2 medium eggplants
Salt
Vegetable oil as needed
  1 large onion, peeled and sliced
  1 pound lean lamb, ground
Freshly ground black pepper to taste
  ½ teaspoon ground cinnamon
  1 tomato, peeled and chopped
  ¼ cup tomato paste
  1 tablespoon chopped fresh parsley
  1 cup milk
  2 tablespoons butter
1½ tablespoons all-purpose flour
  ¼ teaspoon salt
  1 egg yolk, beaten

Peel the eggplants and slice them vertically. Sprinkle the eggplant slices with salt and place in a colander for 30 minutes, allowing the salt to drain water and bitterness from the eggplant. After 30 minutes, rinse the eggplant slices and dry with paper toweling.

Heat 2 tablespoons oil in an ovenproof skillet with a cover. Fry the eggplant slices until golden brown, adding oil as needed. Drain the eggplant slices and reserve.

Combine the onion, lamb, salt and pepper, cinnamon, tomato, tomato paste, and parsley in the skillet. Stir, then cover and convection-bake in a 325-degree oven for 30 minutes.

In a 10 × 6 × 1¾-inch baking dish, or a 1½-quart ovenproof casserole, make layers of eggplant slices and meat mixture, beginning and ending with eggplant. Set aside while you make a béchamel sauce.

Heat the milk until it is almost boiling. Meanwhile, melt the butter in a large saucepan and add the flour. Cook for 2 minutes, stirring constantly.

Off heat, add the milk very gradually to the butter-flour mixture, stirring constantly. Add ¼ teaspoon salt and cook over low heat, until the sauce thickens. Cool the sauce slightly and beat in the egg yolk.

Pour the sauce over the eggplant and convection-bake in a 350-degree oven for 25 to 30 minutes, or until a brown crust has formed and the layers have blended.

Serves: 8

COUNTRY KITCHEN LAMB 'N' BISCUITS

2 tablespoons olive oil
1½ pounds lean, boneless stewing lamb, cut into 1-inch cubes
1 onion, peeled and sliced
2 cloves garlic, peeled and mashed
1 package (10 ounces) frozen tiny lima beans, thawed
2 cups stewed tomatoes, chopped
2 cup beef broth
Salt and freshly ground black pepper to taste
1½ cups biscuit mix
½ cup yellow cornmeal
½ cup milk

Heat the oil in a large skillet and brown the lamb cubes on all sides. Add the onion and garlic and cook an additional 5 minutes, then add the lima beans, tomatoes, beef broth, and salt and pepper and bring to a simmer.

Spoon all the ingredients into a 2-quart ovenproof casserole. Cover and convection-bake in a 350-degree oven for 45 to 55 minutes, or until the lamb is fork tender.

Combine the biscuit mix and cornmeal, then add the milk and mix. On a lightly floured board, knead the biscuit dough ten times. Roll out to a thickness of ½ inch, then cut into 2-inch biscuits and place on top of the lamb stew.

Convection-bake, uncovered, for an additional 15 minutes, or until the biscuits are done.

Serves: 6

LAMB SHANKS ITALIAN

4 lamb shanks
¼ cup olive oil
1 onion, peeled and sliced
3 cloves garlic, peeled and mashed
2 cups beef broth
1 cup tomato sauce
½ teaspoon dried oregano
Salt and freshly ground black pepper to taste

Over medium-high heat, brown the lamb shanks in oil in a skillet, turning the shanks to brown on all sides. Remove the shanks to a 3-quart ovenproof casserole.

In the same skillet, sauté the onion and garlic, stirring, for 5 minutes. Add the broth and tomato sauce to the skillet and bring to a simmer. Pour the sauce over lamb and add the seasonings.

Cover the casserole and convection-cook in a 350-degree oven for 1¾ to 2 hours, or until the meat is tender.

Serves: 4

CASSOULET

Cassoulet is the French answer to Boston baked beans. Depending upon what part of France the recipe comes from, the dish can contain pork, lamb, duck, goose, sausages, or any combination of these meats. The one consistent factor in preparing a cassoulet is the amount of time it takes—hours of preparation go into this delicious dish. But now, thanks to convection-oven cooking, the meats roast while the beans bake, and preparation and cooking time is reduced by many hours. The result? A cassoulet you can be proud of even if you serve it to the most finicky gourmet from France.

1 pound Great Northern beans
½ pound bacon, cut into squares
1 onion, peeled and chopped
6 sprigs parsley, chopped
3 cloves garlic, peeled and mashed
½ teaspoon dried thyme
1 bay leaf
1 cup tomato sauce
1 cup dry white wine
3 cups beef broth
Salt and freshly ground black pepper to taste
6 pork chops
4 shoulder lamb chops
Leftover roast duck or goose (optional)
1 pound French pork garlic sausage or Polish kielbasa sausage

Place the beans in a large saucepan filled with water. Bring to a boil, cook for 2 minutes, and remove from the heat. Allow the beans to soak in the water for 1 hour. Drain the beans and reserve the cooking liquid. Spoon the beans into a 13 × 9 × 2-inch baking pan, or the largest roasting pan that will fit in your convection oven.

Combine all the remaining ingredients, except for the meats, and spoon over the beans; stir well. Add enough cooking liquid so that the beans are almost covered.

Preheat convection oven to Maximum temperature for 10 minutes.

Place the pan with the beans on the floor of the oven and place the pork and lamb chops on the rack above. The chops should be directly over the beans so that the beans will absorb the meat drippings.

Convection-broil the chops for 15 minutes, or until they lose their raw look, then remove the chops and rack from the oven. Wash the rack. Place the chops and the optional duck or goose in the pan with beans. Cover the pan (you may use foil), place it on the rack, and return it to oven.

Lower the temperature to 350 degrees and convection-bake for 2 hours. Uncover, add the sausages, and bake an additional 20 to 30 minutes, or until the sausages are cooked.

Serves: 8

GLAZED PINEAPPLE PORK CHOPS

8 pork chops
Salt and freshly ground black pepper to
   taste
4 sweet potatoes, cooked, peeled, and
   sliced
1 can (16 ounces) pineapple chunks,
   drained and juice reserved
2 tablespoons brown sugar
1 teaspoon prepared mustard
2 tablespoons vinegar
1 tablespoon Worcestershire sauce
2 tablespoons catsup
2 tablespoons cornstarch
½ cup water

Sear the pork chops on both sides in a skillet and then transfer to an ovenproof baking dish with a cover. Season with salt and pepper and arrange the sweet potato slices around and between the chops.

In a saucepan, combine the juice from the canned pineapple with the brown sugar, mustard, vinegar, Worcestershire sauce, and catsup. Bring to a simmer. Dissolve the cornstarch in the water and, off heat, stir into the sauce. Bring the sauce back to a simmer and cook until clear and slightly thickened.

Pour the sauce over the pork chops, cover, and convection-bake in a 325-degree oven for 45 minutes to 1 hour, or until pork is tender. Uncover, add the pineapple chunks, and bake an additional 5 to 10 minutes.

Serves: 4

FIRESIDE PORK AND APPLE CASSEROLE

¼ cup all-purpose flour
1½ teaspoons salt
½ teaspoon freshly ground black pepper
½ teaspoon paprika
2 pounds boneless pork shoulder, cut
   into 2-inch cubes
3 tablespoons vegetable oil
1 large onion, peeled and thinly sliced
1 bay leaf, crumbled
1 teaspoon dried sage
1 clove garlic, peeled and mashed
1 cup apple butter
2 carrots, scraped and sliced
2 stalks celery, trimmed and sliced
2 tart apples, peeled, cored, and sliced
½ cup chicken broth

In a bag, combine the flour, salt, pepper, and paprika. Add the pork cubes and shake well until the pork is covered with the flour mixture. Heat the oil in a large skillet, then add the pork and brown well on all sides. Remove to a 2-quart ovenproof casserole.

Place the onion in the same skillet and cook over low heat until translucent, then add, along with the bay leaf, sage, garlic, and apple butter, to the casserole. Cover and convection-bake in a 325-degree oven for 40 to 45 minutes, or until the pork is tender.

Add the carrots, celery, apples, and chicken broth to the casserole. Cover and cook for 20 to 30 minutes, or until the vegetables and apple are tender.

Serves: 4 to 6

POTATO AND PORK CASSEROLE

6 pork chops, each ½ inch thick
2 onions, sliced and sautéed in butter
3 large potatoes, peeled and thinly sliced
Salt and freshly ground black pepper to taste
1 cup beef broth

Preheat the convection oven to 350 degrees.

Place the onions and potato slices in a shallow baking pan. Season with salt and pepper and pour the beef broth over all, then place the pan in the oven.

Place the chops on the rack and place the rack directly over the pan. Convection-roast for 35 to 45 minutes, or until the meat is cooked and the potatoes are tender.

Serves: 3 to 4

CANTONESE PORK WITH STIR-FRIED VEGETABLES

¼ cup vegetable oil
2 pounds boneless pork shoulder, cut into 1-inch cubes
½ cup cider vinegar
½ cup granulated sugar
1 cup beef broth
1 tablespoon soy sauce
2 tablespoons catsup
¼ teaspoon Worcestershire sauce
2 green onions, chopped
1 cup water chestnuts, sliced
2 stalks celery, trimmed and sliced
1 cup bean sprouts
2 tablespoons cornstarch

Heat half the oil in a large skillet and brown the pork on all sides, then remove to a 2-quart ovenproof casserole.

In a large saucepan, combine the vinegar, sugar, and beef broth. Cook until the sugar dissolves. Add the soy sauce, catsup, and Worcestershire sauce. Mix and bring to a simmer.

Pour the sauce over the pork in the casserole, cover, and convection-cook in a 325-degree oven for 1 to 1¼ hours, or until the pork is thoroughly cooked.

Add the remaining oil to the skillet and stir-fry the vegetables for 2 to 3 minutes; the vegetables should remain crisp. Set the vegetables aside.

Remove ½ cup of sauce from the cooked pork and combine with the cornstarch. Mix thoroughly and return the sauce-cornstarch mixture to the casserole. Add the reserved vegetables, stir, and cook, uncovered, for 10 to 15 minutes, or until the sauce is thick, clear, and all the ingredients are hot.

Serves: 6

SAUSAGE BAKE

1 pound tiny pork sausages
4 sweet potatoes, cooked, peeled and
   sliced
2 large apples, cored and sliced
½ cup firmly packed brown sugar
¼ teaspoon ground cinnamon
1 cup orange juice
2 tablespoons butter

Place sausages directly on the rack of the convention oven.

Place the sweet potato slices in a buttered shallow ovenproof pan. Place the apple slices over and around the potato slices. Sprinkle the brown sugar and cinnamon over all and pour the orange juice into the pan. Dot with the butter.

Place the pan directly beneath the sausages and convection-bake in a 350-degree oven for 20 to 30 minutes, or until the sausages are brown and cooked.

Serves: 4 to 6

TUSCAN VEAL CHOPS WITH MUSHROOMS

4 rib veal chops
¼ cup all-purpose flour
Salt and freshly ground black pepper to
   taste
¼ cup olive oil
1 pound fresh mushrooms, sliced
½ cup dry white wine
½ cup tomato sauce

Dredge the veal chops in the flour and season.

Heat the oil in a skillet and brown the veal chops slowly on both sides, turning frequently. Transfer the chops and all pan juices to an ovenproof casserole. Scatter the mushrooms over and around the chops.

Combine the wine and tomato sauce and pour over the chops, then cover the casserole and convection-bake in a 350-degree oven for 15 to 20 minutes, or until the meat is tender.

Serves: 4

CHICKEN BASQUAISE

This interesting chicken dish is easy to make, but looks elegant when served. The tomatoes and hot pepper add color and spice. The recipe calls for rice cooked *al dente*, or slightly chewy to the bite. The reason is that the rice cooks with the chicken an additional half hour, and if rice is overcooked it becomes an unappetizing mush.

1 chicken (2½ to 3 pounds), quartered
4 tablespoons (½ stick) butter
Salt and freshly ground black pepper to
    taste
2 cups rice, cooked *al dente*
6 tomatoes, quartered
1 hot cherry pepper, seeded and chopped

Brown the chicken in the butter; the chicken should be nicely browned, but only partially cooked. Place the chicken pieces in an ovenproof casserole, season, and spoon the rice over. Pour the pan juices from chicken over rice.

Place the tomato quarters and pepper pieces on the rice, cover, and convection-bake in a 350-degree oven for 30 minutes, or until the chicken is tender.

Serves: 4

CHICKEN AND RICE PAPRIKA

1 onion, peeled and sliced
2 cloves garlic, peeled and mashed
1 cup raw rice
1 tomato, peeled and chopped
¼ cup chopped fresh parsley
Salt, freshly ground white pepper, and
    paprika to taste
2 cups chicken broth
1 chicken (2½ to 3 pounds), cut into
    eight pieces
6 tablespoons butter

Place the onion, garlic, rice, tomato, parsley, salt, pepper, paprika, and chicken broth in the drip pan of the convection oven and stir to combine.

Place the chicken pieces on the rack. Season with salt, pepper, and paprika and dot with the butter. Place the rack directly over the drip pan and convection-bake in a 350-degree oven for 35 to 45 minutes, or until the chicken is cooked and the rice is tender.

Serves: 4

MORNING-AFTER ONION SOUP

You don't really have to wait until the morning after a big party to enjoy this onion soup. It's delicious on any winter's evening, and with the bread, and the quantity of cheeses, it's a meal in itself. *Soupe à l'oignon gratinée* is a great favorite in Paris's famous Pied de Cochon Restaurant, and is served there twenty-four hours every day. If you think you'd like to serve that famous restaurant's version of onion soup, eliminate the béchamel sauce and pour the soup into individual small casseroles before topping with the toasted French bread and cheeses.

5 medium onions, peeled and chopped
¼ cup vegetable oil
4 tablespoons (½ stick) butter
3 tablespoons all-purpose flour
8 cups beef broth
Salt and freshly ground white pepper to taste
10 slices French bread
¼ pound (1 stick) butter, softened
1½–2 cups Béchamel Sauce (page 71)
2 cups grated Swiss cheese
¼ cup freshly grated Parmesan cheese

Sauté the onions in a large saucepan in a combination of the oil and butter, stirring frequently. The onions should be a light golden brown. Add the flour and cook an additional 4 minutes, stirring constantly. Add the beef broth and salt and pepper, then cover the pan and allow the soup to simmer for 15 minutes.

Preheat the convection oven to Maximum temperature for 10 minutes.

While the soup is simmering, butter the French bread slices with the softened butter and place directly on the oven rack. Convection-broil for 5 minutes, or until the bread is slightly toasted and the butter has melted into the bread.

Lower the oven temperature to 350 degrees. Spread the toasted bread with béchamel sauce. Stir the remaining béchamel sauce into the soup. Pour the soup into a 3- or 3½-quart ovenproof casserole, place the bread slices on top, and sprinkle with the grated cheeses. Place the casserole in the convection oven for 15 to 25 minutes, or until the cheese has melted and is slightly brown.

Serves: 8

BÉCHAMEL SAUCE

4 tablespoons (½ stick) butter
3 tablespoons all-purpose flour
2 cups milk
¼ teaspoon salt

Heat the butter in a large saucepan. Add the flour and cook this roux, stirring constantly, for 2 to 3 minutes over low heat.

Heat the milk to the boiling point in another pan, then, off heat, gradually add the milk to butter-flour mixture, stirring constantly. Add the salt.

Over low heat, cook the sauce, stirring, until it thickens. If the sauce is too thick, add a little milk, a tablespoonful at a time. If the sauce is lumpy, beat with an egg beater or wire whisk.

Use the béchamel sauce at once, or keep warm in the top of a double boiler, over hot water, using low heat.

Yield: 1½ to 2 cups

POTAGE BASQUAISE

More than a soup but not quite a stew, this combination of beans, vegetables, ham, and cheese makes a winter's day meal when served with crusty French bread and sweet butter. Fresh fruit and a cheese platter are all you will need for dessert.

2 cups dried lima beans, presoaked and drained
6 turnips, peeled and sliced
5 potatoes, peeled and cubed
½ head white cabbage, cored and shredded
4 carrots, scraped and sliced
2 stalks celery, trimmed and chopped
1 onion, peeled and sliced
1 clove garlic, peeled and mashed
1 ham bone
Salt and freshly ground black pepper to taste
1 cup grated Swiss cheese

Place all the ingredients except for the grated cheese in a 4-quart ovenproof casserole, with water to cover. Cover and convection-cook in a 350-degree oven for 2 hours, or until the beans are tender and the vegetables are cooked. Remove ham bone.

Sprinkle the cheese on top and return to the oven. Turn the heat to 450 degrees, and continue cooking until the cheese melts.

Serves: 8

6
SLOW COOKING

SLOW COOKING RECIPES

Piquant Pot Roast

Juniper Beef Stew

Winter's Day Oxtail Stew

Hot and Spicy Short Ribs

Money-Saver Lamb Dinner

Ossobuco à la Modena

Goulash Soup Hapsburg

Sweet and Pungent Pork Young China

Split Pea Soup Amsterdam

Grandma's Best Bean Soup

Mexican Chicken Molé

Many convection ovens have the facility to slow-cook. This means that you can place a stew, casserole, or soup-as-a-meal in your convection oven and allow it to cook at a low temperature for many hours.

We have found that slow cooking works best at 225 to 250 degrees. Check your oven before slow cooking. It may have a Stay-On position, which means that it will do just that—stay on until you turn it off. Or it may have a timer that you can set by hours. This means if you're using a slow cooking recipe that calls for 6 hours, and your oven turns off after 4 hours, you—or someone—has to turn the oven back on for the additional 2 hours.

Slow cooking is a boon if you have to be away from home for hours at a time. Food that is slow cooked has a subtly different flavor—spices are spicier, and gravies or sauces do not evaporate or cook away.

Slow cooking is especially useful for preparing cheaper but flavorful cuts of meat that are enhanced by long, slow simmering.

PIQUANT POT ROAST

¼ cup vegetable oil
1 brisket of beef (4 to 5 pounds)
1 large onion, peeled and sliced
1 clove of garlic, peeled and mashed
1 cup tomato sauce
2 cups beef broth
¼ teaspoon Tabasco or hot pepper sauce
½ teaspoon Worcestershire sauce
2 carrots, scraped and sliced

Heat the oil in a large skillet and brown the meat on all sides. Remove to a 4-quart ovenproof casserole, then add all the other ingredients, cover, and convection slow-cook at 225 to 250 degrees for 8 to 10 hours, or until the meat is tender.

Serves: 6 to 8

JUNIPER BEEF STEW

3 pounds beef, from the rump, cut into strips approximately 2 × 4 × ½ inches
3 tablespoons vegetable oil
3 large onions, peeled and sliced
2 cloves garlic, peeled and mashed
1 cup beef broth
2 cups light beer
3 tablespoons firmly packed brown sugar
2 teaspoons dried juniper berries
Salt and freshly ground black pepper to taste
2 tablespoons wine vinegar
1½ tablespoons cornstarch

Heat the oil in a large skillet and brown the meat on all sides.

Place all the ingredients, except for the wine vinegar and cornstarch, in a 3-quart ovenproof casserole. Cover and convection slow-cook at 225 to 250 degrees for 8 to 10 hours, or until the meat is tender.

Spoon 1 cup of the liquid from the casserole into a small bowl. Combine the vinegar and cornstarch, mix well, and add to the bowl, stirring. Return to the casserole and let cook, uncovered, at 325 degrees until the sauce has thickened and is clear.

Heat thoroughly before serving.

Serves: 6

WINTER'S DAY OXTAIL STEW

If you've never tried it, oxtail stew might sound strange, but once you've had this exceptionally rich cut of meat you'll become a devotee. And despite its name, oxtail stew is really beef stew.

1 oxtail (have your butcher cut it into serving pieces)
½ cup all-purpose flour
¼ cup olive oil
Salt and freshly ground black pepper to taste
1 onion, peeled and chopped
1 clove garlic, peeled and mashed
3 medium potatoes, peeled and cubed
6 small white onions, peeled
2 carrots, scraped and sliced
1 cup tomato juice
¼ teaspoon Tabasco or hot pepper sauce
1 cup dry red wine
1 bay leaf

Roll the oxtail pieces in the flour. Heat the oil in a large skillet and brown the oxtail pieces, turning them from side to side to brown thoroughly. Season with salt and pepper, then, using a slotted spoon, remove to a 3-quart ovenproof casserole.

Sauté the onion and garlic in the same skillet and add to the casserole, along with the potatoes, white onions, and carrots.

Combine all other ingredients in a small bowl, mix well, and pour over meat in the casserole. Cover and convection slow-cook at 225 to 250 degrees for 6 to 8 hours, or until the meat is tender.

Serves: 2 to 3

HOT AND SPICY SHORT RIBS

4 pounds short ribs
2 cups tomato juice
1 cup beef broth
1 onion, peeled and diced
2 cloves garlic, peeled and mashed
¼ cup chili powder
3 tablespoons firmly packed brown sugar
½ cup vinegar
¼ teaspoon hot pepper flakes
Salt to taste

Brown the short ribs in a skillet (no oil is needed because they will render their own fat as they brown); then, using a slotted spoon, remove to a 3-quart oven-proof casserole.

Combine all the other ingredients in a large bowl and mix thoroughly, then pour the sauce over the ribs, cover the casserole, and convection slow-cook at 225 to 250 degrees for 6 to 8 hours, or until the meat is tender.

Serves: 6 to 8

MONEY-SAVER LAMB DINNER

Leg of lamb and lamb chops are expensive, and may be only once-in-a-while treats, but lamb shanks are flavorful and one of the most neglected meats in American cookery. Take a tip from smart European cooks and serve lamb shanks. They're simple to prepare and kind to the budget. And the nicest thing about them is that they don't taste as though you were trying to save money—they just taste delicious.

¼ cup vegetable oil
4 lamb shanks
Salt and freshly ground black pepper to taste
2 onions, peeled and sliced
1 carrot, scraped and sliced
1 green pepper, seeded and cut into strips
1 cup dry red wine
1 cup beef broth
1 tomato, peeled and chopped
¼ teaspoon red pepper flakes

Heat the oil in a large skillet and brown the lamb shanks, turning the shanks from side to side to brown thoroughly. Season with salt and pepper, then remove to a 3-quart ovenproof casserole.

Add all the other ingredients to the skillet and bring to a simmer, stirring from time to time, then pour the contents of the skillet over the lamb, cover, and convection slow-cook at 225 to 250 degrees for 8 hours, or until the lamb is tender.

Serve with a rice pilaf.

Serves: 4

OSSOBUCO À LA MODENA

¼ cup olive oil
4 veal shanks
¼ cup all-purpose flour
Salt and freshly ground black pepper to taste
3 strips lemon rind
½ cup dry white wine
4 sprigs Italian parsley
½ cup chopped Italian plum tomatoes
¼ teaspoon dried thyme
1 bay leaf

Heat the oil in a large skillet. Roll the veal shanks in the flour, season with salt and pepper, and brown in the oil. Remove from the skillet and place in a 3-quart ovenproof casserole. Add the remaining ingredients to the skillet and bring to a simmer. Pour over the meat.

Cover the casserole and convection slow-cook at 225 to 250 degrees for 8 to 10 hours, or until the meat is tender.

Serve with rice.

Serves: 4

GOULASH SOUP HAPSBURG

2 pounds meaty veal or beef bones
6 cups beef broth
2 carrots, scraped and diced
2 onions, peeled
Bouquet garni, tied in a cheesecloth bag
    (2 bay leaves, ¼ teaspoon dried
    thyme, 5 sprigs parsley, 8 whole
    peppercorns, leaves from 2 stalks
    celery, 2 cloves garlic, ½ teaspoon
    caraway seeds)
Salt to taste
2 tomatoes, peeled, seeded, and
    chopped
3 tablespoons vegetable shortening
1 onion, peeled and minced
2 green peppers, seeded and chopped
2 tablespoons all-purpose flour
2 cups peeled and cubed potatoes
¼ cup tomato sauce

Combine the beef or veal bones, beef broth, carrots, onions, bouquet garni, salt, and tomatoes in a 4-quart ovenproof casserole. Cover and convection slow-cook at 225 to 250 degrees for 6 hours.

Remove the bones from the casserole and shred the meat. Strain the soup, discarding the vegetables and bouquet garni, and return the shredded meat and soup to the casserole.

Melt the shortening in a large skillet, then add the onion and peppers and cook, stirring, until the vegetables are wilted. Sprinkle with the flour and continue cooking, stirring all the time, for 5 minutes. Add the potatoes and tomato sauce to the skillet and cook, stirring, for an additional 5 minutes.

Add the mixture to the soup in the casserole, then cover and continue to convection slow-cook for 3 to 4 hours, or until the potatoes are cooked.

Serves: 8 to 10

SWEET AND PUNGENT PORK YOUNG CHINA

2 tablespoons vegetable oil
2 pounds boneless pork shoulder, cut
    into 1-inch cubes
1 can (8 ounces) pineapple chunks,
    drained, juice reserved
¼ cup white vinegar
¼ cup firmly packed brown sugar
2 tablespoons soy sauce
2 tablespoons catsup
¼ teaspoon ground ginger
¼ teaspoon Tabasco or hot pepper
    sauce
1½ tablespoons cornstarch
1 green pepper, seeded and cut into
    strips
2 carrots, scraped and sliced

Heat the oil in a large skillet and brown the pork on all sides, then, using a slotted spoon, remove to a 2-quart ovenproof casserole.

Pour the reserved pineapple liquid into the skillet. Add the vinegar, brown sugar, soy sauce, catsup, ginger, and Tabasco. Mix thoroughly and bring to a simmer.

Pour the sauce over pork, cover the casserole, and convection slow-cook at 225 to 250 degrees for 6 to 8 hours, or until the pork is tender.

Remove ½ cup of sauce from the casserole and stir in the cornstarch, mixing well. Return the sauce-cornstarch mixture to the casserole and add the pineapple chunks, green pepper, and carrots. Stir, then cook, uncovered, for 15 to 30 minutes, or until the sauce is clear and thick and all the ingredients are hot.

Serves: 6

SPLIT-PEA SOUP AMSTERDAM

1 large ham hock or 2 ham bones
1 pound split peas, presoaked and
   drained
2 quarts water
1 teaspoon salt
½ teaspoon freshly ground black pepper
2 bay leaves
2 stalks celery, trimmed and chopped
1 large onion, peeled and minced
¼ teaspoon dried thyme

Combine all the ingredients in a 4-quart ovenproof casserole. Cover and convection slow-cook at 225 to 250 degrees for 6 to 8 hours.

Remove the ham hock or bones from the soup and cut off the meat. Shred the meat and return to the casserole. Stir well, then place the casserole in the oven again and heat thoroughly for an additional 15 to 20 minutes at 325 degrees.

Serves: 8

GRANDMA'S BEST BEAN SOUP

1 pound dried kidney beans, presoaked
   and drained
2 quarts water
2 to 3 ham bones or 1 ham hock
1 onion, peeled and pierced with 3
   cloves
½ cup chopped celery leaves
2 cloves garlic, peeled and mashed
2 bay leaves
¼ teaspoon dried thyme
1 tomato, peeled, seeded, and chopped
Salt and freshly ground black pepper to
   taste

Place all the ingredients in a 4-quart ovenproof casserole. Cover and convection slow-cook at 225 to 250 degrees for 8 to 10 hours, or until the beans and ham are tender and the soup is thick.

Remove the bones from casserole. Cut off the meat, shred, and return the meat to the casserole. Sir well, then place the casserole in the oven again, and heat thoroughly at 325 degrees for an additional 15 to 20 minutes.

Serves: 10

MEXICAN CHICKEN MOLÉ

If you've never tried *molé*, the idea of chicken in a chocolate-flavored sauce may sound strange. But try it once and you'll become an *aficionado* of this dish. The chocolate is just one of the many ingredients that go into the sauce, and as the recipe calls for unsweetened chocolate, the sauce is not one bit sweet.

Serve the *molé* with steamed rice and a green salad garnished with orange segments.

2 chickens (2½ to 3 pounds each) cut into eight pieces
6 tablespoons vegetable oil
Salt to taste
1½ cups chicken broth
¾ teaspoon anise seeds
1 tablespoon sesame seeds
3 cloves garlic, peeled
⅛ teaspoon ground cloves
¼ cup dark raisins
⅓ cup blanched almonds, toasted
⅛ teaspoon ground coriander
1 square unsweetened chocolate, grated
2 tomatoes, peeled
2 each hot and mild chili peppers, seeded and chopped (see note)

Brown the chicken pieces in the oil, turning to brown on all sides, then remove to a 3-quart ovenproof casserole.

Mix all the other ingredients together in a food processor or blender (you may have to do this in two or three batches). Blend thoroughly, until the ingredients become a smooth sauce.

Pour the sauce over the chicken, then cover and convection slow-cook at 225 to 250 degrees for 5 to 7 hours, or until the chicken is tender.

Serves: 8

Note:
Chili peppers both hot and mild may be purchased canned. The can will indicate whether the peppers are hot or mild.

7
SHASHLIK, KEBABS, AND DISHES EN BROCHETTE

SHASHLIK, KEBABS, AND DISHES EN BROCHETTE

Czar's Shashlik

Rice Pilaf

East Indian Kebab

Raita

Saucy Kebabs

Hot Dog Kebabs 'n' Baked Beans

Tokyo Seafood Kebabs

Polynesian Rumaki

Bombay Chicken Kebabs

Beef Burgundy en Brochette

Cubes of meat, alternating with vegetables, threaded on a skewer, and broiled. There's something especially appealing to the appetite about these dishes. Whether you call them *kebabs* as they do in the Mideast, *shashlik* as they're known in Russia, or *en brochette* as in France, just about everyone likes food prepared this way.

Up till now you may have used your kebab skewers only on an outdoor barbecue. Bring them back into the house, and start convection kebabing!

All convection ovens can be used for cooking food on a skewer, and at this time there is one convection oven manufacturer that offers a shish kebab accessory. If you have the accessory, fine—if not, use your own skewers and place them directly on a shallow, ovenproof baking pan. Because the dish will prevent the air from circulating completely around the skewered meat, the cooking time will be increased slightly over the oven with the shish kebab accessory.

CZAR'S SHASHLIK

1 pound boneless leg of lamb, cut into
  1-inch cubes
1 clove garlic, peeled and mashed
½ cup olive oil
Salt and freshly ground black pepper to
  taste
½ tablespoon dried basil, crushed
2 large onions, peeled and quartered

Place the lamb cubes in a bowl. Combine the garlic, olive oil, salt, pepper, and basil. Mix well and pour over the lamb. Marinate overnight.

Preheat the convection oven to Maximum temperature for 10 to 20 minutes.

Thread the lamb and onion quarters on 4 skewers. If using the shish kebab accessory, place the skewers into the kebab rack, then pour the marinade over; or place the skewers in a single layer on a shallow, ovenproof baking pan and pour the marinade over. Convection-broil for 15 to 18 minutes, or until the lamb is tender.

Serve with Rice Pilaf (see below).

Serves: 4

RICE PILAF

4 tablespoons (½ stick) butter
3 green onions, minced
1 cup raw rice
2 cups chicken broth
Salt and freshly ground white pepper to
  taste

Melt the butter in a skillet and sauté the green onions for 3 minutes, stirring. Add the rice to the skillet and continue cooking until the rice grains have a milky look. Spoon the rice into a 1½-quart ovenproof casserole.

Bring the chicken broth to a simmer and pour over the rice. Season to taste, then cover the casserole and convection-bake in a 325-degree oven for 20 to 25 minutes, or until the liquid is absorbed and the rice is tender. If serving with Shashlik, this may be heated in the convection oven for 10 minutes while the Shashlik cooks.

Serves: 4

EAST INDIAN KEBAB

1 pound lean lamb, ground
1 garlic clove, peeled and mashed
¼ cup grated onion
1 egg, lightly beaten
1 teaspoon ground cumin
1 tablespoon catsup
½ teaspoon curry powder
½ cup breadcrumbs
2 onions, peeled and quartered

Preheat the convection oven to Maximum temperature for 10 to 20 minutes. Have ready 4 skewers.

Combine all the ingredients, except for the quartered onions. Mix until thoroughly blended, then divide the meat mixture into 8 portions. Form into thick, sausagelike patties around the skewers, alternating with the onion quarters. (Each of the skewers should hold 2 kebabs and 2 onion quarters.)

If using the shish kebab accessory, place the skewers into the kebab rack; or place the skewers in a single layer on a shallow, ovenproof baking pan. Convection-broil for 10 minutes, or until the meat is brown and cooked.

Serve with Raita (see below).

Serves: 4

RAITA

This tangy yogurt and cucumber sauce is delicious with East Indian Kebab or with plain shish kebab that has not been cooked in a sauce. It can also be served as a side dish with leg of lamb.

2 cups plain yogurt
1 cucumber, peeled and grated
1 small onion, peeled and grated
1 teaspoon ground cumin
Salt and freshly ground white pepper to
    taste

Combine all the ingredients, mixing thoroughly. Chill before serving.

Serves: 4 to 6

SAUCY KEBABS

1 pound lean lamb, cut into 1-inch cubes
2 green peppers, each seeded and cut into quarters
8 large mushroom caps
2 tomatoes, quartered
Salt and freshly ground black pepper to taste
1 cup tomato sauce
¼ teaspoon Tabasco or hot pepper sauce
¼ teaspoon dried rosemary
1 teaspoon Worcestershire sauce

Preheat the convection oven to Maximum temperature for 10 to 20 minutes.

Alternate the meat, green pepper pieces, mushroom caps, and tomato quarters on 4 skewers. Season with salt and pepper.

Combine all the other ingredients in a bowl, mixing well.

If using the shish kebab accessory, place the skewers into the kebab rack, then spoon the sauce over; or place the skewers in a single layer on a shallow, oven-proof baking pan and pour the sauce over. Convection-broil for 15 to 18 minutes, or until the lamb is tender.

Serves: 4

HOT DOG KEBABS 'N' BAKED BEANS

Franks and beans for supper sound like pretty standard fare, but they become something new and interesting when presented the following way!

1 can (16 ounces) cannellini beans, drained
1 onion, peeled and thinly sliced
1 cup tomato sauce
3 tablespoons chopped fresh parsley
¼ teaspoon freshly ground black pepper
6 large frankfurters, cut into 1¼-inch chunks

Preheat the convection oven to Maximum for 10 to 20 minutes.

Combine all the ingredients, except for the frank-furters, mixing thoroughly. Spoon the bean mixture either into a shallow, ovenproof baking dish or directly into the drip pan.

Thread the frankfurter pieces on 4 skewers. If using a shish kebab accessory, place the skewers into the kebab rack over the top of the beans; or place the skewers in a single layer on a shallow, ovenproof baking pan, over the bean pan. Convection-broil for 10 minutes, or until the beans and frankfurters are thoroughly hot.

Serves: 4

TOKYO SEAFOOD KEBABS

1 cup soy sauce
¼ cup dry sherry
½ teaspoon ground ginger
½ pound large sea scallops
½ pound shrimp, shelled and deveined

Thoroughly combine the soy sauce, sherry, and ginger and marinate the scallops and shrimp in the mixture for 1 hour.

Preheat the convection oven to Maximum for 10 to 20 minutes.

Alternately thread the scallops and shrimps on 4 skewers. If using the shish kebab accessory, place the skewers into the kebab rack and then spoon the marinade over; or place the skewers in a single layer on a shallow, ovenproof baking pan and pour the marinade over. Convection-broil for 10 minutes, or until the scallops and shrimp are tender.

Serve with the pan juices and plain, steamed rice.

Serves: 2 to 3

POLYNESIAN RUMAKI

1 pound chicken livers
1 can (8½ ounces) water chestnuts
¼ pound sliced bacon, cut into strips

Preheat the convection oven to Maximum for 10 to 20 minutes.

Wrap the livers and water chestnuts in bacon strips and thread on 6 skewers. If using the shish kebab accessory, place the skewers into the kebab rack; or place the skewers in a single layer on a shallow, ovenproof baking pan. Convection-broil for 20 to 25 minutes, or until the livers and bacon are brown and crisp.

Serves: 6

BOMBAY CHICKEN KEBABS

2 whole chicken breasts, skinned, boned, and cut into 1½-inch pieces
6 tablespoons melted butter
1 teaspoon curry powder
½ teaspoon ground coriander
¼ teaspoon ground turmeric
2 tomatoes, quartered
2 green peppers, each seeded and cut into 8 strips

Place the chicken pieces in a bowl. Combine the butter, curry powder, coriander, and turmeric. Mix well, then spoon over the chicken and marinate for 2 to 4 hours, turning from time to time.

Preheat the convection oven to Maximum temperature for 10 to 15 minutes.

Thread the marinated chicken pieces, tomato and green pepper pieces on 4 skewers. If using the shish kebab accessory, place the skewers into the kebab rack, then spoon the sauce over; or place the skewers in a single layer on a shallow, ovenproof baking pan and pour the sauce over. Convection-broil for 10 to 15 minutes, or until the chicken is tender.

Serves: 4

BEEF BURGUNDY EN BROCHETTE

1 pound boneless sirloin, rump, or shoulder steak, cut into 1-inch cubes
2 tablespoons olive oil
1 cup dry red wine
½ teaspoon dried thyme
1 bay leaf, crushed
Salt and freshly ground black pepper to taste
8 large mushroom caps
4 small white onions, peeled

Place the beef cubes in a bowl. Combine all the other ingredients except for the mushroom caps and onions. Mix well, pour over beef, and let the meat marinate for 4 to 6 hours.

Preheat the convection oven to Maximum temperature for 10 to 20 minutes.

Thread the beef cubes, mushrooms, and onions on 4 skewers. If using the shish kebab accessory, place the skewers into the kebab rack, then pour the marinade over; or place the skewers in a single layer on a shallow, ovenproof baking pan and pour the marinade over. Convection-broil for 10 to 15 minutes, or until the beef is tender.

Serve with the pan juices.

Serves: 4

8
VEGETABLES PLUS

VEGETABLES PLUS

Whole Stuffed Cabbage

Baked Saffron Rice with Peppers

Stuffed Green Peppers

Twice-Baked Potatoes With Cheese

Potato-Ham Scallop

Ham, Egg, and Potato Hash

Potatoes Niçoise

Traditional Jansson's Temptation

Spinach and Potato Mousse

Sweet Potato Surprise

Irene's Baked Acorn Squash

Mrs. Halsey's Spaghetti Squash

Filled Tomatoes

Tomatoes Provençale

Zucchini with Cheese and Basil

Stuffed Zucchini

Zucchini Florentine

There are many pluses to vegetables prepared in a convection oven. Vegetable dishes that are baked in this manner have infinitely more character than vegetables that have been steamed or boiled.

Baked vegetables also combine with meats and other foods and can be presented as a main course, not only as a side dish.

You can cook great quantities of vegetables in your convection oven. The cooking time needed will not be multiplied by the amount of food cooked. Whether you bake one potato or ten, the time remains 45 minutes—which is not true for microwave ovens.

Too often people have been turned away from vegetables by being lectured on how good vegetables are for them—they're low in calories, comparatively inexpensive, rich with vitamins and minerals. That's all true, but best of all they can be delicious when prepared with imagination.

Vegetables are pretty, too. The scarlet of a stuffed tomato, the dark green of a stuffed pepper, the brown crust of a twice-baked potato—all add color as well as flavor to a meal. (And they're good for you, too!)

WHOLE STUFFED CABBAGE

1 head (2 pounds) cabbage
1 onion, peeled and grated
2 tablespoons vegetable oil
1 pound ground beef
½ cup raw rice
1 egg, beaten
½ cup breadcrumbs
1 cup tomato sauce
Salt and freshly ground black pepper to taste
2 cups beef broth

Place the cabbage in boiling, salted water and parboil for 5 minutes. Drain the cabbage and allow to cool.

Turn the cabbage upside down and cut out the core, then turn right side up and gently pull the cabbage leaves apart from the center until there is a hollow. Set the cabbage aside.

In a large skillet, sauté the onion in the oil. Add the ground beef and rice and cook, stirring, for 10 to 15 minutes, or until the meat has lost its raw, red look. Add the egg, breadcrumbs, ½ cup of the tomato sauce, and the seasonings to the meat. Mix well.

Remove one large outside leaf from the cabbage and reserve. Stuff the meat mixture into the hollowed center of the cabbage and place the reserved leaf over the top of the filling. Carefully tie the cabbage around with butcher's twine so that it holds its shape, then place in an ovenproof casserole.

Combine the beef broth and remaining tomato sauce and pour over the cabbage.

Cover the casserole and convection-bake in a 350-degree oven for 1 hour and 10 minutes to 1 hour and 20 minutes, until the cabbage is tender and the meat is cooked.

Serves: 6

BAKED SAFFRON RICE WITH PEPPERS

6 tablespoons olive oil
2 green peppers, seeded and cut in strips
1 onion, peeled and chopped
3 cloves garlic, peeled and mashed
1 cup raw rice
2 cups chicken broth
Pinch of saffron
¼ teaspoon white pepper
Pinch of cayenne pepper (optional)

Heat the olive oil in an ovenproof skillet with a lid and sauté the peppers, onion, and garlic, stirring, for 3 minutes. Add the rice to the skillet and continue to cook and stir until the rice has lost its milky look.

Heat the chicken broth in a small saucepan and stir in the saffron, white pepper, and cayenne. Pour the broth over the rice and bring to a boil. Cover the skillet and convection-bake in a 325-degree oven for 20 minutes, or until the rice is tender and the liquid is absorbed.

Serves: 4

STUFFED GREEN PEPPERS

6 green peppers
1 pound ground beef
1 onion, peeled and minced
1 clove garlic, peeled and mashed
1 egg, beaten
⅓ cup raw rice
Salt and freshly ground black pepper to taste
2 tablespoons butter
1 tablespoon all-purpose flour
2 cups tomato sauce
1 cup water
2 teaspoons granulated sugar, or more to taste
¼ teaspoon hot red pepper flakes

Cut the tops from the green peppers, then remove the ribs and seeds from the insides, wash, and drain.

Combine the beef, onion, garlic, egg, and rice. Mix thoroughly, then season. Fill the peppers seven-eighths full with the meat mixture and place in an ovenproof casserole.

Heat the butter in a saucepan and add the flour. Cook, stirring, for about 1 minute, or until the flour is a pale brown color. Off heat, gradually stir in the tomato sauce, then add the water. Bring the sauce to a simmer and add the sugar and hot pepper flakes.

Pour the sauce over and around the green peppers. Cover the casserole and convection-bake in a 350-degree oven for 45 to 50 minutes, or until the peppers are tender.

Serves: 6

TWICE-BAKED POTATOES WITH CHEESE

4 medium baking potatoes
½ cup milk
2 tablespoons butter
½ cup grated Cheddar cheese
1 package (3 ounces) cream cheese
¼ teaspoon freshly ground white pepper
¼ teaspoon salt

Convection-bake the potatoes directly on the rack in a 350-degree oven for 40 to 45 minutes.

Cut 1 inch off the top of each baked potato. Scoop out the potato pulp, being careful not to break the shells. In a large mixing bowl, combine the pulp with all the other ingredients and mix thoroughly.

Spoon the mixture back into the shells and convection-bake for 15 to 20 minutes, or until brown on top.

Serves: 4

POTATO-HAM SCALLOP

3 tablespoons butter
2 tablespoons all-purpose flour
2 cups milk
½ teaspoon salt
¼ teaspoon freshly ground white pepper
4 large potatoes, peeled and sliced
½ pound boiled ham, diced
4 tablespoons (½ stick) butter

Melt the butter in a large saucepan. Stir in the flour and cook, stirring, for 3 minutes. Gradually add the milk, stirring constantly. Add the seasonings and continue cooking, stirring, until the sauce is smooth and thick.

Arrange the potatoes and ham in one layer in an ovenproof casserole. Pour the sauce over all, dot with butter, and convection-bake in a 350-degree oven for 35 to 45 minutes, or until the potatoes are tender and the top is crusty.

Serves: 4 to 6

HAM, EGG, AND POTATO HASH

If you're looking for a perfect Sunday night supper dish, here it is. It's a complete meal in itself, or you can serve it as a side dish with chops or chicken.

Choose a meat or chicken recipe and let your convection oven cook your entire meal. Place the meat or chicken in the oven 10 or 15 minutes earlier—depending on the recipe you use—and then place the hash dish in the oven. You'll save both time and energy if you use your convection oven to cook more than one course at a time.

1 green pepper, seeded and diced
¼ pound (1 stick) butter
¼ pound boiled ham, diced
4 eggs, lightly beaten
2 shallots, peeled and minced
2 green onions, chopped
½ cup heavy sweet cream
Salt and freshly ground white pepper to taste
4 large potatoes, peeled and grated

Sauté the green pepper in half the butter until translucent. Stir in the ham and cook, stirring, for 3 additional minutes.

Combine the eggs, shallots, green onions, and cream and beat until well mixed. Add the pepper-ham combination to the egg mixture and season. Spoon the grated potatoes into the egg mixture and mix thoroughly.

Generously butter a shallow ovenproof baking dish and spoon the egg-potato mixture into it. Dot with the remaining butter and convection-bake in a 350-degree oven for 20 to 30 minutes, or until the potatoes are tender and the top is crusty.

Serves: 4

POTATOES NIÇOISE

4 large baking potatoes
4 tablespoons (½ stick) butter
2 hard-boiled eggs, chopped
½ cup tomato sauce
4 rolled fillets of anchovies with capers, mashed
8 pitted black olives, sliced
¼ cup tuna packed in olive oil, drained and mashed
2 green onions, minced
Salt and freshly ground black pepper to taste

Convection-bake the potatoes in a 400-degree oven, directly on the rack, for 45 minutes, or until the potatoes are tender.

Cut the potatoes in half lengthwise and scoop out the potato pulp, being very careful not to tear the shells. Mash the pulp with the butter and gradually add all the other ingredients, mixing thoroughly.

Spoon the potato mixture back into both halves of the potato shells and place in a shallow ovenproof dish. Convection-bake in a 325-degree oven for 15 to 20 minutes, or until the potatoes are hot and slightly crusted on top.

Serves: 8

TRADITIONAL JANSSON'S TEMPTATION

2 leeks, white part only, well cleaned and sliced
6 tablespoons butter
1 pound potatoes, peeled and cut into narrow strips
1 can (2 ounces) flat fillets of anchovies
Salt and freshly ground white pepper to taste
1 cup heavy sweet cream

Sauté the leeks in half the butter, stirring, until they are transparent.

Butter a shallow ovenproof baking dish with 1 tablespoon of the butter. Place half the potatoes in the baking dish and top with the leeks. Place the anchovies on top of the leeks, then top with the rest of the potatoes. Dot with the remaining 2 tablespoons butter and season with salt and pepper.

Convection-bake in a 350-degree oven for 10 minutes. Add half the cream and return to the oven. Bake for another 10 minutes, then add the remainder of the cream and bake for an additional 30 minutes, or until the potatoes are tender.

Serves: 4 to 6

SPINACH AND POTATO MOUSSE

1 package (10 ounces) frozen chopped
  spinach, thawed
4 large potatoes
¼ pound (1 stick) butter, softened
¼ cup sour cream
1 egg, lightly beaten
Salt and freshly ground black pepper to
  taste
Pinch of freshly grated nutmeg

Cook the spinach thoroughly and drain; peel the potatoes, cut into quarters, and cook until tender.

Mash the potatoes and add to the spinach. Mix thoroughly, adding butter until the spinach and potatoes are thoroughly combined and the butter is absorbed. Stir in the sour cream, mixing once again, then stir in the egg and seasonings until all the ingredients are thoroughly combined.

Spoon the spinach-potato mixture into an ovenproof casserole and convection-bake in a 350-degree oven for 20 to 30 minutes, until the mousse is hot and the top is lightly browned.

Serves: 4

SWEET POTATO SURPRISE

4 large sweet potatoes
½ cup light cream
1 egg, lightly beaten
¼ pound (1 stick) butter
¼ teaspoon ground cardamom

Convection-bake the potatoes directly on the rack in a 350-degree oven for 45 minutes, or until tender.

Cut the potatoes in half lengthwise and scoop out the potato pulp, being careful to leave the shells intact. Combine the pulp with the cream, egg, butter, and cardamom, mixing thoroughly.

Pile the potato mixture back into both halves of the potato shells. Turn the heat down to 325 degrees and convection-bake for 15 to 20 minutes, or until the potatoes are hot and a light brown crust has formed on top.

Serves: 8

IRENE'S BAKED ACORN SQUASH

2 acorn squash
4 tablespoons butter
4 tablespoons dark brown sugar
8 tablespoons orange juice
Freshly ground white pepper to taste

Cut the squash in half and scoop out the seeds. Place 1 tablespoon butter, 1 tablespoon sugar, and 2 tablespoons orange juice in each squash half. Season with pepper.

Place the squash halves on a baking sheet and convection-bake in a 350-degree oven for 45 to 50 minutes, or until the squash is tender.

Serves: 4

MRS. HALSEY'S GREEN THUMB SPAGHETTI SQUASH

For many people who are dieting, spaghetti squash is the answer to those times when they yearn for spaghetti but are trying to avoid the calories in pasta.

Spaghetti squash is a large, oblong, yellow vegetable, and after it's cooked the strands within bear a visual resemblance to strands of spaghetti. It is becoming more popular and well known around the country as pasta lovers happily serve it with their favorite spaghetti sauce. It's also a favorite with vegetable lovers because of its delicious and unique flavor.

1 spaghetti squash (approximately 2 to 2½ pounds)
3 tablespoons vegetable oil
¼ cup melted butter
Salt and freshly ground black pepper to taste
Marinara sauce, or other spaghetti sauce of your choice

Pierce the unpeeled spaghetti squash with a fork in three or four places and brush with oil. Place the squash directly on the rack and convection-bake in a 325-degree oven for 45 minutes, or until the squash is easily pierced with a fork.

Remove the squash from the oven and cut it in half lengthwise. Discard the seeds and scoop out the vegetable "spaghetti" strands into a large skillet. Toss with the butter and season.

Add marinara sauce, or your favorite spaghetti sauce, and heat thoroughly before serving.

Serves: 4

FILLED TOMATOES

6 large, ripe but firm tomatoes
2 tablespoons olive oil
1 small onion, peeled and minced
½ teaspoon dried oregano
1 pound lamb, ground
¼ teaspoon dried rosemary
1 egg, lightly beaten
½ cup breadcrumbs
¼ teaspoon salt
Freshly ground black pepper to taste

Cut a small slice off the top of each of the tomatoes and carefully scoop out the tomato pulp from inside. Reserve both pulp and shells.

Heat the oil in a large skillet and sauté the onion until translucent. Add the tomato pulp and oregano to the skillet and cook for 15 minutes, stirring occasionally, then pour the sauce into the bottom of an ovenproof dish and set aside.

Combine the meat and all the other ingredients, mixing thoroughly. Stuff the tomatoes with the meat mixture, then place the stuffed tomatoes in the ovenproof dish, on top of the sauce.

Convection-bake in a 350-degree oven for 20 to 30 minutes, basting occasionally with the sauce.

Serves: 6

TOMATOES PROVENÇALE

4 large, ripe but firm tomatoes
Salt and freshly ground black pepper to taste
½ cup breadcrumbs
2 cloves garlic, peeled and mashed
2 tablespoons chopped Italian parsley
¼ cup olive oil

Carefully cut a slice off the tops of the tomatoes and reserve.

Combine all the other ingredients and carefully spoon the mixture on top of each tomato. Cover the crumb-topped tomatoes with the reserved tomato slices.

Place the tomatoes in a buttered baking dish and convection-bake at 325 degrees for 15 to 20 minutes.

Serves: 4

ZUCCHINI WITH CHEESE AND BASIL

1 medium onion, peeled and minced
2 tablespoons butter
2 pounds zucchini
3 eggs
½ cup grated Swiss cheese
2 tablespoons chopped fresh basil
Salt and freshly ground white pepper to taste

Sauté the onion in the butter until translucent.

Wash and trim the zucchini. Slice and place in an ovenproof dish. Add onions.

Beat the eggs; add the cheese, basil, and salt and pepper. Pour the egg mixture over the zucchini slices and convection-bake in a 325-degree oven for 20 minutes, or until the top is lightly browned.

Serves: 4

STUFFED ZUCCHINI

¼ cup olive oil
1 onion, peeled and grated
1 clove garlic, peeled and mashed
1 pound ground beef
½ cup raw rice
Salt and freshly ground black pepper to taste
4 medium zucchini
3 cups stewed tomatoes, chopped
1 tablespoon granulated sugar
½ hot cherry pepper, minced (optional)

Heat the oil in a large skillet and sauté the grated onion and the garlic, stirring, for 3 minutes. Add the beef, rice, and salt and pepper and continue cooking until the onion and meat are lightly browned.

Wash and trim the zucchini. Cut them in half lengthwise, then scoop out the centers and reserve. Fill the zucchini halves with the meat-rice mixture.

Chop the reserved zucchini pulp and combine with the chopped stewed tomatoes, sugar, and hot pepper to make a sauce. Mix well, then pour one-half of the sauce into the bottom of an ovenproof dish.

Place the zucchini halves on top of the sauce and pour the remainder of the sauce over.

Convection-bake in a 350-degree oven for 20 to 30 minutes.

Serves: 4

ZUCCHINI FLORENTINE

4 medium zucchini

1 package (10 ounces) frozen chopped spinach, thawed

7 tablespoons (1 stick less 1 tablespoon) butter

1 egg, lightly beaten

2 tablespoons freshly grated Parmesan cheese

1 clove garlic, peeled and mashed

Salt and freshly ground black pepper to taste

½ cup breadcrumbs

Wash and trim the zucchini.

Cut the zucchini in half lengthwise, and using a small melon ball scoop, scoop out the zucchini pulp, creating hollowed zucchini halves. Reserve the pulp and place the zucchini halves in a buttered shallow ovenproof baking dish.

Combine the cooked spinach with the zucchini pulp and 4 tablespoons of the butter. Using a food processor or food mill, puree the spinach-zucchini combination, then add the egg, cheese, garlic, and salt and pepper, mixing well.

Spoon the vegetable mixture into the zucchini halves and sprinkle with the breadcrumbs. Dot with the remaining butter and convection-bake in a 350-degree oven for 20 to 30 minutes, or until the zucchini is tender.

Serves: 4

9
PASTA AND NOODLES

PASTA & NOODLES

Pastitsio Idra

Noodles Pudding

Spicy Ziti Casserole

Noodles Budapest

Fettucine with Walnuts

Old-Fashioned Macaroni and Cheese

Macaroni Shells and Shrimp

Baked Orzo and Chicken Livers

Is there anyone who doesn't love pasta? The wonder of pasta and noodles of all shapes and sizes is how marvelously they combine with cheese, meat, and seafood. Noodles and pasta are a delicious way of stretching a small amount of protein into a complete main course.

And pasta and noodles take on additional flavor and texture when baked in a convection oven. The top becomes crisp and crusty, while the noodles beneath meld warmly with the other ingredients.

Pasta and noodle dishes can be presented as a main course, as a side dish, or as a dessert! Here are recipes in each flavorful category.

PASTITSIO IDRA

½ pound ziti or elbow macaroni
6 tablespoons butter
1 large onion, peeled and minced
1 pound ground beef
1 cup tomato sauce
Salt and freshly ground black pepper to
     taste
¼ teaspoon dried thyme
⅛ teaspoon freshly grated nutmeg
1 tablespoon all-purpose flour
1 cup milk
¼ cup heavy sweet cream
1 egg yolk, beaten
⅓ cup freshly grated Parmesan cheese

Cook the pasta until it is *al dente,* or firm to the bite. Drain and set aside.

Heat half the butter in a large skillet and sauté the onion until translucent but not brown. Add the beef and cook, stirring, until it has lost its raw, red look. Add the tomato sauce, salt and pepper, thyme, and nutmeg. Cook for 10 minutes, stirring.

In a saucepan, melt the remaining butter. Add the flour and cook, stirring, for 2 minutes. Gradually add the milk and cook, stirring, until the mixture is thick and smooth.

In a bowl, combine the cream and egg yolk, blending well. Off heat, stir the cream–egg yolk mixture into the flour-milk mixture. Heat thoroughly over low heat, stirring constantly.

Place a layer of cooked pasta in a baking dish, then cover with a layer of meat. Alternate pasta and meat, finishing with meat. Pour the cream-egg sauce on top and sprinkle with the grated cheese.

Convection-bake in a 325-degree oven for 25 to 30 minutes, or until the top is brown and the sauce is bubbly.

Serves: 4 to 6

NOODLE PUDDING

½ pound broad egg noodles, cooked and
     drained
6 tablespoons melted butter
3 eggs, lightly beaten
½ cup firmly packed brown sugar
1 teaspoon ground cinnamon
2 cups milk
¼ cup raisins
1 apple, cored and chopped

Toss the egg noodles with 3 tablespoons of the melted butter. Set aside.

In a large bowl, combine all the other ingredients, mixing thoroughly. Add the noodles to bowl and toss in the sauce, until all the ingredients are combined.

Turn the noodle mixture into a buttered 2-quart ovenproof casserole and convection-bake in a 350-degree oven for 30 to 40 minutes, or until the pudding is set.

Serves: 4

SPICY ZITI CASSEROLE

1 pound ziti or other tubular pasta,
  cooked *al dente* and drained
4 tablespoons olive oil
1 pound hot Italian sausage, cut into
  small pieces
1 onion, peeled and grated
4 cups stewed Italian plum tomatoes,
  chopped
Salt to taste
¼ teaspoon hot pepper flakes
½ cup pitted black olives, sliced

Place ziti in a 13 × 9 × 2-inch baking dish and spoon 2 tablespoons of the olive oil over it. Set aside.

Heat 1 tablespoon of the oil in a skillet and cook the sausage pieces, browning thoroughly on all sides. When the sausage is almost cooked, add the onion to the skillet and continue cooking, stirring. Add the tomatoes, salt, pepper flakes, and olives to the skillet and bring the sausage-sauce mixture to a simmer.

Pour the sauce over the ziti and stir to mix thoroughly. Spoon the remaining 1 tablespoon of olive oil over the ziti and convection-bake in a 325-degree oven for 25 to 30 minutes.

Serves: 4 to 6

NOODLES BUDAPEST

Traditionally, this dish is prepared with *szalonna*, the twice-smoked Hungarian bacon that is sold in pork stores in those cities which have Hungarian neighborhoods. If *szalonna* is not available in your area, regular bacon works almost as well.

¼ pound *szalonna* or bacon
1 pound medium-wide egg noodles,
  cooked and drained
¼ pound (1 stick) butter, melted
1 pound pot cheese
½ pint sour cream

In a skillet, fry the *szalonna* or bacon until crisp. Drain and break into small pieces. Do not crumble, or the pieces will be too small.

Pour the butter over the cooked noodles, and toss. Add the bacon and mix. Combine the pot cheese and sour cream and spoon over the noodles, tossing once again.

Turn the noodle-cheese mixture into a 2-quart ovenproof casserole and convection-bake in a 350-degree oven for 15 to 20 minutes, or until the noodles and sauce are hot and the noodles on top are slightly crispy.

Serves: 4 to 6

FETTUCINE WITH WALNUTS

1 pound fettucine, cooked and drained
¼ pound (1 stick) butter, melted
1½ cups walnut pieces
½ cup granulated sugar, or more to taste
½ teaspoon grated lemon rind

Toss the fettucine with half the melted butter and turn into a 2-quart ovenproof casserole. Set aside.

In a bowl, combine the walnut pieces, sugar, and lemon rind. Mix well and add more sugar if desired.

Toss the fettucine with the walnut-sugar combination and spoon the remainder of the butter on top. Convection-bake in a 350-degree oven for 15 to 20 minutes, or until the fettucine is hot and slightly crispy on top.

This may be served as a dessert or as a side dish with duck or goose.

Serves: 4 to 6

OLD-FASHIONED MACARONI AND CHEESE

½ pound elbow macaroni, cooked *al dente* and drained
2 tablespoons butter
1 onion, peeled and chopped
1 clove garlic, peeled and mashed
1 cup milk
6 ounces sharp Cheddar cheese, grated
2 ounces Swiss cheese, grated
1 tablespoon chopped fresh parsley
Salt and freshly ground white pepper to taste
Pinch of cayenne pepper

Butter a 9-inch square baking pan and spoon the cooked elbow macaroni into it. Set aside.

Heat the butter in a large skillet, and sauté the onion and garlic until translucent. Pour the milk into the skillet and cook, stirring, until the mixture comes to a simmer.

Add the cheeses to the skillet and continue cooking, stirring, until the milk-cheese mixture is thick and blended. Off heat, add the parsley and seasonings.

Pour the cheese sauce over macaroni and mix. Convection-bake in a 350-degree oven for 20 to 30 minutes, or until a brown crust has formed on top and the macaroni is piping hot.

Serves: 4 to 6

MACARONI SHELLS AND SHRIMP

4 tablespoons (½ stick) butter
3 tablespoons all-purpose flour
2 cups milk
½ teaspoon salt
¼ teaspoon freshly ground white pepper
1 tablespoon vinegar
3 tablespoons chopped parsley
1 pound cooked, cleaned shrimp
½ pound small macaroni shells (also known as *maruzzelle*), cooked *al dente* and drained

Heat the butter in a large saucepan. Stir in the flour and cook, stirring, for 3 minutes. Gradually stir in the milk, and continue cooking, stirring, until the sauce is smooth and thick. Off heat, stir in the seasonings, vinegar and parsley.

Add the shrimp and combine thoroughly, then pour the shrimp and sauce over the cooked pasta shells and turn into a 2-quart ovenproof casserole. Convection-bake in a 350-degree oven for 15 to 20 minutes.

Serves: 4

BAKED ORZO AND CHICKEN LIVERS

Orzo is a tiny rice-shaped pasta. If you can't find orzo, any other small pasta can be substituted in this recipe.

1 pound orzo or other tiny pasta, cooked and drained
¼ pound (1 stick) butter, melted
1 pound chicken livers
Paprika
1 cup chicken broth
½ cup heavy sweet cream
Salt and freshly ground black pepper to taste
¼ cup chopped fresh parsley

Toss the orzo with half the melted butter and turn into a 2-quart ovenproof casserole. Set aside.

Cut the chicken livers in half, dust liberally with paprika, and sauté in the remaining butter in a large skillet. Turn the liver halves to brown on all sides.

Fold the livers into the orzo and pour the chicken broth over all. Stir in the heavy cream, season with salt and pepper, and stir in parsley, then cover the casserole and convection-bake in a 350-degree oven for 15 minutes, or until the orzo and livers are hot.

Serves: 6 to 8

10
SOUFFLÉS AND PANCAKES

SOUFFLÉS AND PANCAKES

Chocolate Soufflé

Lemon Soufflé

Salmon Soufflé

Ham and Cheese Soufflé

Grand Marnier Soufflé

Pennsylvania Dutch Pancake

Orange Puff Pancake

Sunday Breakfast Pancake

Use your convection oven to prepare everyone's favorite—soufflé! Whether it's a dessert soufflé or a soufflé as a main dish, everyone loves to see—and eat—these lighter-than-air creations. Just remember that a soufflé waits for no one—so let your guests enjoy the anticipation. Make sure that everyone is seated at the table, fork and spoon poised, before you bring this delicacy to the table. Soufflés collapse with disappointment if they're not eaten immediately.

Because of the constantly circulating hot air, you may place a soufflé anywhere in a convection oven, but if you have a very small oven, make sure the soufflé has room to rise.

The puffed pancakes in this chapter are easier to cope with. They, too, will fall, if not eaten immediately, but they don't have as far to go. Puffed pancakes baked in a convection oven are a deliciously different way to present a Sunday breakfast. They also save the cook from standing over a hot stove, flipping flapjacks endlessly.

CHOCOLATE SOUFFLÉ

8 ounces Baker's German sweet
   chocolate, broken into small pieces
1 tablespoon instant coffee
5 tablespoons water
2 tablespoons butter
⅓ cup all-purpose flour
2 cups milk
½ teaspoon vanilla extract
4 eggs, separated, plus 2 egg whites
Pinch of salt
½ cup granulated sugar

Preheat the convection oven to 350 degrees for 5 to 10 minutes. Butter the bottom and sides of a 2-quart soufflé dish and add a 2-inch foil collar.

Combine the chocolate, instant coffee, and water in the top of a double boiler and cook, stirring, over simmering water until the mixture is completely smooth. Set aside.

Melt the butter in a saucepan. Add the flour and milk, stirring with a wire whisk until smooth, then add the vanilla and cook over medium heat, stirring constantly, until the mixture is thick and smooth.

Blend the chocolate mixture into the butter-flour combination and remove from the heat.

Lightly beat the egg yolks and stir gradually into the chocolate mixture. Beat the 6 egg whites with a pinch of salt, gradually adding the sugar, until the egg whites are stiff.

Fold the egg whites gently into the chocolate mixture, then pour the soufflé mixture into the prepared dish and convection-bake for 30 to 35 minutes, or until a toothpick inserted into the side of the puff comes out dry.

Remove the collar and serve at once.

Serves: 6

LEMON SOUFFLÉ

1½ teaspoons grated lemon peel
3 tablespoons lemon juice
⅓ cup granulated sugar
¼ teaspoon salt
5 tablespoons butter
4 eggs, separated
¼ teaspoon cream of tartar

Preheat the convection oven to 350 degrees for 5 to 10 minutes. Butter a 1½-quart soufflé dish and sprinkle the bottom and sides with sugar; add a 2-inch foil collar.

In a medium saucepan, combine the lemon peel and juice, sugar, and salt and beat until well blended. Add the butter and cook, stirring constantly, over medium-high heat until the mixture boils. Boil, stirring constantly, for 1 minute, then remove from the heat.

In small mixing bowl, beat the egg yolks at high speed until thick and lemon colored, about 5 minutes. Blend a little of the hot mixture into the yolks, then stir the yolk mixture into the hot lemon mixture.

In a large mixing bowl, beat the egg whites and cream of tartar at high speed until the whites are stiff but not dry. Gently but thoroughly fold the yolk mixture into the whites, then carefully pour into the prepared dish. Convection-bake for 30 to 35 minutes, or until a toothpick inserted into the side of the puff comes out dry.

Remove the collar and serve at once.

Serves: 6

SALMON SOUFFLÉ

2 tablespoons freshly grated Parmesan cheese
2 tablespoons chopped green onion
4 tablespoons butter
3 tablespoons all-purpose flour
1 cup milk
Salt
¼ teaspoon freshly ground white pepper
1 tablespoon catsup
5 eggs, separated
1 can (7¾ ounces) salmon, drained
2 ounces grated Swiss cheese

Preheat the convection oven to 350 degrees for 5 to 10 minutes. Butter a 1½-quart soufflé dish and sprinkle bottom and sides with the grated Parmesan cheese.

In a large saucepan, sauté the green onion in the butter, stirring, until the onion is translucent. Add the flour and cook for 1 minute, stirring constantly. Add the milk, ½ teaspoon salt, the pepper, and catsup and cook, stirring with a wire whisk, until the mixture is thickened. Remove from the heat and add the egg yolks, one by one, beating after each addition. Add the salmon and half of the grated cheese. Mix thoroughly.

Beat the egg whites with a pinch of salt until stiff. Gradually fold the whites into the salmon mixture, then pour into the prepared soufflé dish and sprinkle with the remaining Swiss cheese. Convection-bake for 35 to 40 minutes, or until the top is well browned and puffy and a toothpick inserted in the side of the puff comes out dry.

Serve at once.

Serves: 4 to 5

HAM AND CHEESE SOUFFLÉ

1 small onion, finely chopped
2 ounces ham, diced
½ cup diced mushrooms
4 tablespoons (½ stick) butter
2 tablespoons all-purpose flour
1 teaspoon salt
¼ teaspoon freshly ground white pepper
1 cup milk
1 cup grated Cheddar cheese
½ cup grated Swiss cheese
1 tablespoon freshly grated Parmesan cheese
¼ teaspoon Dijon-type mustard
4 eggs, separated

Preheat the convection oven to 350 degrees for 5 to 10 minutes. Butter a 2-quart soufflé dish.

In a skillet, sauté the onion, ham, and mushrooms in 2 tablespoons of the butter until the onion is translucent and the ham and mushrooms are slightly brown. Set aside.

Melt the remaining butter in a large saucepan and stir in the flour, salt, and pepper. Gradually add the milk and cook, stirring constantly, until the mixture comes to a boil and thickens. Stir in the onion mixture and add all the cheeses gradually, continuing to stir until the mixture is well blended and cheeses are thoroughly melted. Remove from heat and stir in the mustard and egg yolks, mixing well.

Beat the egg whites until stiff, then gently fold the whites into the flour-cheese mixture. Pour the mixture into the prepared dish and convection-bake for 30 to 40 minutes, or until a toothpick inserted into the side of the puff comes out dry.

Serve at once.

Serves: 4

GRAND MARNIER SOUFFLÉ

3 tablespoons butter
3 tablespoons all-purpose flour
¾ cup milk
4 eggs, separated, plus 2 egg whites
3 tablespoons orange marmalade
¼ cup Grand Marnier

Preheat the convection oven to 350 degrees for 5 to 10 minutes. Butter a 1½-quart soufflé dish and sprinkle the bottom and sides with sugar; add a 2-inch foil collar.

Melt the butter in a saucepan and stir in the flour. Add the milk gradually, stirring with a wire whisk, and cook over low heat until the mixture thickens. Lightly beat the egg yolks, then stir in, along with the marmalade; add the Grand Marnier.

Beat the 6 egg whites until stiff and fold them into the soufflé mixture, then pour the mixture into the prepared dish and convection-bake for 30 to 35 minutes, or until a toothpick inserted into the side of the puff comes out dry.

Remove the collar and serve at once.

Serves: 4

PENNSYLVANIA DUTCH PANCAKE

3 eggs
½ cup milk
¼ cup all purpose-flour
1 tablespoon granulated sugar
½ teaspoon salt
1 tablespoon butter
1 cup apple compote or applesauce

Combine the eggs, milk, flour, sugar, and salt, then, using an egg beater or an electric mixer, beat until smooth.

Put the butter in a 9-inch pie plate and place in a 375-degree convection oven until it melts, then pour the pancake mixture into the pie plate and convection-bake for 12 to 15 minutes, or until the pancake is puffy and brown.

While the pancake is baking, heat the apple compote or applesauce. Spoon the hot apples over the pancake and serve at once.

Serves: 2

ORANGE PUFF PANCAKE

3 eggs
½ cup milk
½ cup pancake mix
2 tablespoons butter
Grated zest of 1 orange
2 large oranges, peeled, seeded, and cut
  into bite-sized pieces
½ cup firmly packed light brown sugar
½ teaspoon ground cinnamon

Using an egg beater or electric mixer, beat the eggs until foamy. Beat in the milk, then gradually beat in the pancake mix until the combination is completely smooth.

Put the butter in a 9-inch pie plate and place in a 375-degree convection oven until the butter melts.

While the butter is melting, continue beating the pancake mixture, gradually adding the orange zest. Pour the mixture into the pie plate and convection-bake for 12 to 15 minutes, or until the pancake is puffy and brown.

Combine the orange pieces, brown sugar, and cinnamon and spoon over the pancake. Serve at once.

Serves: 4

SUNDAY BREAKFAST PANCAKE

¼ cup all-purpose flour
½ cup milk
2 eggs, lightly beaten
1 teaspoon grated lemon rind
4 tablespoons (½ stick) butter
2 tablespoons superfine granulated sugar
3 tablespoons orange marmalade

Combine the flour, milk, eggs, and lemon rind. Using an egg beater, beat lightly, allowing the batter to remain a little lumpy.

Put the butter in a 9-inch pie plate and place in a 375-degree convection oven. When the butter has melted, pour in the pancake batter and convection-bake for 12 to 15 minutes, or until the pancake is puffy and lightly brown.

Remove the pie plate from the oven and sprinkle with the sugar. Return to the oven for 3 minutes, then spread the marmalade on top and serve.

Serves: 2

11
PIES AND QUICHES

PIES AND QUICHES

Pâte Brisée for Pastry Shells

Bacon-Mushroom Quiche

Spinach Quiche

Homemade Pizza

Tomato and Olive Pie

Orange Custard Pie

Apple-Walnut Pie

Favorite Walnut Fudge Pie

Lenke's Cream Cheese Pie

CONVECTION BAKING

Commercial bakers have been using convection ovens for years, and now you can enjoy this method of professional baking in your own home. Here are the guidelines:

TEMPERATURE

When adapting your own recipes, lower the temperature by 25 to 50 degrees. This was the suggestion of most manufacturers, though one did recommend a lowering of 75 degrees for yeast-risen dough, while another said to bake at conventional temperatures.

The recipes in this section, on the average, call for temperatures 50 degrees lower than those used in conventional baking.

TIME

Time is approximately one-third less when convection baking. However, you can save even more time by baking as many pies or trays of cookies as your oven will hold. Heat is uniform—or almost—throughout a convection oven, which means you don't have to worry about centering pies or cookies.

PREHEATING

Most manufacturers recommended preheating, while one did not. We found that preheating was necessary in some recipes, but not in all, as can be seen in this section and others that include baking recipes.

UTENSILS

You can use any standard, ovenproof baking pans that will fit in your convection oven. Just remember that metal conducts heat better than glass. Shiny metal pans reflect heat and are best when used for cakes, muffins, and cookies. Dark metal pans absorb heat and are better for heavier doughs and pastries, such as breads and pies.

FROZEN PIES AND PASTRIES

In most cases, preheating is not necessary. Follow all other package directions, except where the oven manufacturer specifically recommends lowering temperature, and check time ten minutes before the end of suggested cooking time.

FOR A CRISPIER CRUST ON BREADS

If you prefer a heavier, crispier crust on breads, place a pan of hot water on the floor of the oven and place the bread pan on the rack over the hot water.

PÂTE BRISÉE (FOR PARTIALLY BAKED PIE CRUSTS OR PASTRY SHELLS)

INGREDIENTS FOR A SINGLE 9-INCH PIE CRUST

1⅓ cups all-purpose flour
½ teaspoon salt
¼ pound (1 stick) butter
3 to 4 tablespoons ice water

INGREDIENTS FOR A DOUBLE PIE CRUST

2¼ cups all-purpose flour
½ teaspoon salt
¼ pound plus 4 tablespoons butter (1½ sticks)
4 to 5 tablespoons ice water

To prepare pâte brisée in a food processor:
Place all the ingredients except the ice water in the food processor. Process until mixture has the consistency of coarse meal. With the machine running, add the water gradually to the processor. Continue processing until the mixture forms a ball; then refrigerate for ½ hour.

To prepare pâte brisée by hand:
In a small bowl combine the flour and salt. Cut the butter into the flour, using a pastry blender or two knives, until the particles are the size of small peas. Sprinkle water over the flour, 1 tablespoon at a time, and stir with a fork until lightly moistened. Form into a ball, and refrigerate for 30 minutes.

To partially bake pâte brisée single 9-inch pie shell:
Preheat the convection oven to 375 degrees for 5 to 10 minutes.

Roll out the dough on a lightly floured board and fit into a 9-inch pie plate. Prick the dough with a fork. Fit a piece of aluminum foil into the crust and weight with aluminum nuggets or dried beans.

Convection bake for 7 minutes (the pastry should be somewhat set, but still soft). Remove the aluminum liner and nuggets or beans. Prick the dough again and return to the oven for 2 minutes.

Allow the pie shell to cool for 10 minutes before filling.

Yield: 1 nine-inch partially baked pie shell

Variations
For a cream cheese pie shell: Use 4 tablespoons (½ stick) butter plus 2 ounces cream cheese for a single 9-inch pie shell.

For a Cheddar cheese pie shell: Use 4 tablespoons (½ stick) butter and ¼ cup grated Cheddar cheese for a single 9-inch pie shell.

BACON-MUSHROOM QUICHE

8 slices bacon
1 medium onion, peeled and chopped
¼ pound mushrooms, sliced
4 eggs, beaten
1 cup heavy cream
2 tablespoons grated Parmesan cheese
6 ounces Swiss cheese, grated
¼ teaspoon freshly ground black pepper
1 nine-inch pie shell, partially baked (see page 125)

Fry the bacon until crisp. Drain and crumble, then set aside. Sauté the onion and mushrooms in the bacon drippings until the vegetables are limp.

In a large mixing bowl, combine the eggs, cream, cheeses, and pepper. Add the bacon, onion, and mushrooms to the egg mixture, then pour into the pie shell. Convection-bake in a 325-degree oven for 30 to 40 minutes, or until a knife inserted 1 inch from the center comes out dry.

Serves: 6

SPINACH QUICHE

8 slices bacon
1 medium onion, peeled and chopped
4 eggs, beaten
¾ cup heavy cream
2 tablespoons grated Parmesan cheese
6 ounces cheese (Swiss, Cheddar, Gruyère, or your favorite combination), grated
1 tablespoon all-purpose flour
1 package (10 ounces) frozen chopped creamed spinach, thawed
1 nine-inch single pie shell, partially baked (see page 125)

Fry the bacon until crisp. Drain and crumble, then set aside. Sauté the onion in the bacon drippings until limp.

In a large mixing bowl, combine the eggs, cream, cheeses, flour and spinach. Add the bacon and onion to the egg mixture and pour mixture into the pie shell. Convection-bake in a 325-degree oven for 30 to 40 minutes, or until a knife inserted 1 inch from the center comes out dry.

Serves: 6

HOMEMADE PIZZA

At last! Pizza you don't have to go out for. Real pizza, not the make-do kind based on an English muffin or French bread, and not the commercial frozen variety, either, but real, homemade pizza! Why not? Pizzerias have been using convection ovens for years.

1 package (¼ ounce) active dry yeast
¾ cup lukewarm water (105 degrees to 115 degrees)
¼ teaspoon sugar
2 to 2½ cups all-purpose flour
1 teaspoon salt
1 tablespoon vegetable oil
1 cup tomato sauce
4 ounces mozzarella cheese, grated
2 tablespoons freshly grated Parmesan cheese
1 teaspoon dried oregano
¼ teaspoon garlic salt

TOPPING

Your favorite combination: sliced green peppers, sautéed onions, sliced mushrooms, pepperoni slices, anchovies

Sprinkle the yeast over the warm water, then add the sugar and stir to dissolve. Allow to stand for 5 to 8 minutes; the mixture should bubble and grow. If it does not, the yeast is dead; begin again.

In a large mixing bowl, combine 1½ cups of the flour, the salt, yeast mixture, and oil. Work in the remaining flour, then knead on a lightly floured board until the dough is smooth and elastic, about 8 minutes. Place the dough in a lightly greased bowl, cover, and allow to rise in a warm, draft-free place for 2 to 3 hours, or until doubled in bulk.

Preheat the convection oven to Maximum for 5 to 10 minutes. Sprinkle cornmeal on a cookie sheet. Stretch dough onto the cookie sheet and bake for 10 minutes.

Remove the dough from the oven. Spoon on the tomato sauce, then sprinkle with the cheeses, oregano, garlic salt, and any combination of the topping ingredients.

Return the pizza to the oven and bake for an additional 5 to 10 minutes, or until the crust is brown and the top is melted and bubbly.

Serves: 3 to 4

TOMATO AND OLIVE PIE

2 tablespoons vegetable oil
1 small onion, peeled and chopped
1 pound tomatoes, peeled and sliced
1 tablespoon chopped fresh parsley
3 eggs, beaten
⅓ cup stuffed green olives, halved
¾ cup grated Gruyère cheese
¼ teaspoon dried oregano
Salt and freshly ground black pepper to
  taste
1 nine-inch pastry shell, partially baked
  (see page 125)

Heat the oil in a large skillet and sauté the onion until translucent. Add the tomato slices and parsley and continue cooking, stirring, for 5 minutes. (Don't worry if the tomato slices break up.) Allow to cool.

Combine the eggs, olives, ½ cup of the cheese, oregano, and salt and pepper. Mix well, then add to the skillet, combining all the ingredients.

Pour the contents of the skillet into the pie shell, sprinkle with the remaining cheese, and convection-bake in a 325-degree oven for 30 to 40 minutes, or until a knife inserted in the center comes out dry.

Serves: 6

ORANGE CUSTARD PIE

1 nine-inch pastry shell (see page 125),
  unbaked
4 eggs, lightly beaten
¾ cup granulated sugar
1½ cups light cream, scalded
2 teaspoons grated orange rind
2 cups orange juice
2 oranges, peeled and divided into
  segments
1½ teaspoons cornstarch

Preheat the convection oven to 350 degrees for 5 to 10 minutes. Brush the pastry shell with a little of the beaten eggs and chill.

Combine the remaining eggs with the sugar and cream. Add the orange rind and 1⅓ cups of the orange juice. Stir, then pour the mixture into the chilled pastry shell and convection-bake for 25 to 35 minutes, or until a knife inserted into the custard comes out dry.

Arrange the orange segments over the custard and set aside while you prepare the following glaze:

Combine the remainder of the orange juice and the cornstarch in a small saucepan. Stir thoroughly, then cook over low heat until thick. Pour over the pie and chill before serving.

Serves: 6

APPLE-WALNUT PIE

PASTRY

2¼ cups all-purpose flour
½ teaspoon salt
1 tablespoon granulated sugar
6 ounces (1½ sticks) butter
4 to 5 tablespoons ice water

FILLING

8 large, tart apples, peeled, cored, and sliced
½ cup raisins
½ cup chopped walnuts
¾ cup granulated sugar
2 tablespoons maple syrup
2 tablespoons all-purpose flour
2 teaspoons lemon juice
1 teaspoon ground cinnamon
¼ teaspoon freshly grated nutmeg
2 tablespoons butter

Prepare the pastry first. In a small mixing bowl, combine the flour, salt, and sugar. Cut the butter into the flour, using a pastry blender or two knives, until the particles are the size of small peas. Sprinkle water over the mixture, 1 tablespoon at a time, mixing with a fork until the dough is slightly moist. Form the dough into a ball, then divide in half. Roll one half out on a lightly floured board and fit into a 9-inch pie plate.

In a large mixing bowl, combine all the filling ingredients except for the butter. Toss well to combine, then spoon into the pie shell. Dot with the butter.

Roll out the second half of the dough, then cover the filling with it; seal and crimp the edges. Make several slits in the top of the pie to allow steam to escape. Convection-bake in a 375-degree oven for 40 to 45 minutes, or until the crust is golden brown.

Serves: 8

FAVORITE WALNUT FUDGE PIE

1½ squares unsweetened chocolate
1 tablespoon butter
1 cup light corn syrup
¼ cup granulated sugar
¼ teaspoon salt
3 eggs, lightly beaten
1 teaspoon vanilla extract
1 nine-inch pie shell (see page 125), unbaked
½ cup walnut halves

In the top of a double boiler, melt the chocolate and butter. Add the corn syrup, sugar, and salt and bring to a simmer, stirring constantly over low heat. Allow to cool slightly, then gradually add the eggs, stirring constantly, until the mixture is thoroughly blended. Add the vanilla.

Pour the chocolate mixture into the unbaked pie shell and place the walnut halves on top. Convection-bake in a 325-degree oven for 30 to 35 minutes, or until the center is set.

Serves: 6

LENKE'S CREAM CHEESE PIE

This dessert is easy to make, but it's so delicious that everyone will think you've made elaborate preparations. One thing that gives it a more delicate flavor is its shell, made of sweetened pastry. The pastry can be easily prepared in a food processor, or it can be made almost as easily in the conventional manner. Directions for both are given here, as are directions for partially baking the pastry shell.

INGREDIENTS FOR 9-INCH SWEET
PASTRY SHELL

1⅓ cups all-purpose flour
Pinch of salt
 1 tablespoon sugar
 ¼ pound (1 stick) butter, cut into 6 pieces
 2 to 3 tablespoons ice water

INGREDIENTS FOR FILLING

 ½ pound cream cheese
 ¼ pound (1 stick) butter
 ⅔ cup sugar
 2 eggs, lightly beaten
 1 teaspoon grated lemon rind

To prepare pastry in a food processor:
Place all ingredients except ice water in food processor. Process until mixture has the consistency of coarse meal. With the machine running, add water to the processor. Continue processing until mixture forms a ball. Refrigerate for ½ hour.

To prepare pastry by hand:
In a small bowl combine flour, salt and sugar. Cut butter into flour using a pastry cutter, or two knives, until particles are the size of small peas. Add water, 1 tablespoon at a time, until pastry is slightly moist. Form into a ball. Refrigerate for ½ hour.

To partially bake pastry shell:
Preheat convection oven to 375 degrees.
Roll out dough on a lightly floured board and fit into a 9-inch pie plate. Prick dough with a fork. Fit a piece of aluminum foil into crust, and weight with aluminum nuggets or dried beans.
Convection-bake for 7 minutes. Pastry should be somewhat set, but still soft. Remove aluminum liner and nuggets or beans. Prick pastry again and return to oven for 2 minutes. Allow pastry to cool for 10 minutes before filling.

To prepare filling:
Lower convection oven temperature to 300 degrees.
Combine cheese, butter, and sugar in a bowl and mix thoroughly. Gradually beat in eggs and lemon rind. Mix well.
Spoon cheese mixture into pastry shell and convection-bake for approximately ½ hour, or until cheese is slightly brown and puffed and a knife inserted in center comes out dry.
May be served hot or cold.

Serves: 6

12
BREADS AND BISCUITS

BREADS AND BISCUITS

Corn Squares

Apricot Muffins

Popovers

Scones

Spoon Bread

Cranapple Bread

Date 'n' Banana Bread

Sweet Potato Biscuits

Potato Biscuits

Cheese Biscuits

Honey-Wheat Bread

Cuban Bread

Corn Rye Bread

Pumpernickel Raisin Bread

Cottage Cheese Bread

CORN SQUARES

½ cup cornmeal
½ cup all-purpose flour
½ teaspoon baking soda
 1 tablespoon baking powder
 1 teaspoon salt
 5 slices bacon
 1 medium onion, peeled and finely
   chopped
 1 can (16 ounces) cream-style corn
½ cup milk
 2 eggs
½ cup grated Cheddar cheese

Preheat the convection oven to 300 degrees for 5 to 10 minutes.

Combine the cornmeal, flour, baking soda, baking powder, and salt and set aside.

In a large skillet, fry the bacon until crisp. Drain and crumble, then set aside.

Sauté the onion in the bacon grease until limp, then return the bacon to the pan; do not drain off the grease. Add the corn, milk, eggs, and cheese to the skillet and stir in flour mixture.

Pour the batter into a well-buttered 9-inch-square pan and convection-bake for 40 to 50 minutes, or until the bread is brown. (The squares should be moist.)

Serve warm. Delicious with chicken and barbecue dinners.

Serves: 4 to 6

APRICOT MUFFINS

1 cup all-purpose flour
¼ cup granulated sugar
2 teaspoons baking powder
¼ teaspoon salt
1 egg, beaten
½ cup milk
½ cup sour cream
2 tablespoons vegetable oil
½ cup dried apricots, chopped

Preheat the convection oven to 325 degrees for 5 to 10 minutes.

Combine the dry ingredients in a small bowl. In a large bowl, combine the remaining ingredients, then add the flour mixture. Mix until just combined.

Fill well-buttered muffin tins two-thirds full. Convection-bake for 15 to 20 minutes, or until the muffins are lightly browned.

Yield: 8 muffins

POPOVERS

1 cup all-purpose flour
¼ teaspoon salt
2 eggs
1 cup milk
2 tablespoons melted butter

Preheat the convection oven to 375 degrees for 5 to 10 minutes. Butter well a muffin tin or 6 to 8 custard cups.

Sift together the flour and salt. Beat in the eggs, milk, and butter.

Heat the buttered muffin tins or custard cups in the convection oven for 3 minutes, then pour in the batter to three-quarters level and convection-bake for 25 to 30 minutes, or until the popovers are well-puffed and golden. Prick the top of each popover while still in the oven to allow steam to escape, then bake for an additional 5 minutes.

Remove the popovers from tins or custard cups immediately, or the bottoms will become soggy.

Yield: 6 to 8 popovers

SCONES

1½ cups all-purpose flour
1 cup rolled oats
½ teaspoon salt
1 teaspoon baking soda
2½ teaspoons baking powder
1 tablespoon sugar
½ cup raisins (optional)
1 tablespoon butter
1 egg, beaten
¾ cup buttermilk

Preheat the convection oven to 350 degrees for 5 to 10 minutes. Butter well a 9-inch pie plate.

Combine the dry ingredients with the raisins, then cut in the butter with a fork. Combine the egg and buttermilk and add to the dry ingredients, stirring well to combine.

Spoon the mixture into the well-buttered pie plate. Spread with a knife. Score the top with a knife into 6 triangles, then convection-bake for 15 to 20 minutes, or until light brown.

Serves: 6

SPOON BREAD

3 cups milk
1½ cups white cornmeal
4 tablespoons (½ stick) butter
1 teaspoon salt
2 teaspoons baking powder
4 eggs, separated

Heat 2 cups of the milk in a heavy saucepan. Gradually stir in the cornmeal, then add the butter and salt and cook over very low heat for 5 minutes, stirring constantly. Cool until lukewarm, about 20 minutes.

Preheat the convection oven to 300 degrees for 5 to 10 minutes. Butter a 2-quart ovenproof casserole.

Dissolve the baking powder in the remaining milk and beat, along with the egg yolks, into the cornmeal mixture. Beat the egg whites until stiff and fold into cornmeal mixture, then pour into the buttered casserole and bake for 30 to 40 minutes, or until well puffed and brown.

Serves: 6

CRANAPPLE BREAD

2 cups all-purpose flour
1 cup granulated sugar
2 teaspoons baking powder
1 teaspoon salt
½ teaspoon baking soda
¼ cup vegetable oil
1 egg, beaten
1 cup apple juice or cider
¾ cup fresh cranberries, coarsely chopped
1 large, tart apple, cored, peeled and coarsely chopped
½ cup chopped nuts

Preheat the convection oven to 300 degrees for 5 to 10 minutes. Butter well an 8¼ × 4½ × 2½-inch loaf pan.

Combine the dry ingredients in a small bowl. In a large bowl, combine the remaining ingredients. Stir the dry ingredients into this mixture until blended.

Pour the batter into the well-buttered loaf pan and convection-bake for 45 to 50 minutes, or until a toothpick inserted in the center comes out dry.

Yield: 1 loaf

DATE 'N' BANANA BREAD

1¾ cups all-purpose flour
2 teaspoons baking powder
¼ teaspoon baking soda
¼ teaspoon salt
⅔ cup granulated sugar
1 cup chopped dates
⅓ cup vegetable oil
2 eggs, beaten
1 cup mashed, ripe banana
¼ cup milk

Preheat the convection oven to 300 degrees for 5 to 10 minutes. Butter and flour an 8½ × 4½ × 2½-inch loaf pan.

Combine the dry ingredients, mixing well; toss the dates in the mixture. In a separate bowl, combine the oil, eggs, mashed banana, and milk, then stir into the dry ingredients.

Spoon the batter into the buttered and floured loaf pan and convection-bake for 45 to 55 minutes, or until a toothpick inserted in the center comes out dry.

Yield: 1 loaf

SWEET POTATO BISCUITS

2 cups all-purpose flour
5 teaspoons baking powder
1 teaspoon salt
¼ cup granulated sugar
2 cups cooked, mashed sweet potatoes
¼ cup melted butter
½ to ¾ cup milk

Preheat the convection oven to 350 degrees for 5 to 10 minutes. Lightly butter a cookie sheet.

Combine the flour, baking powder, salt, and sugar. Add the potatoes, butter, and enough milk to make a soft dough that can be rolled.

Knead the dough on a lightly floured board until smooth, about 20 times. Roll out to a thickness of ½ inch and cut into rounds with a 1½-inch biscuit cutter.

Place the biscuits on the lightly buttered cookie sheet and convection-bake for 15 to 20 minutes, or until the tops begin to brown slightly. Serve warm.

Yield: Approximately 16 biscuits

POTATO BISCUITS

3 medium potatoes, peeled and cooked
5 tablespoons melted butter
1½ cups all-purpose flour
½ teaspoon salt
4 teaspoons baking powder
2 tablespoons granulated sugar
½ cup milk

Preheat the convection oven to 350 degrees for 5 to 10 minutes. Butter a cookie sheet.

Mash the potatoes with the butter. Combine the dry ingredients and add to the potatoes. Mix well. Add the milk and mix again.

Turn the mixture onto a lightly floured board and knead 20 times. Flatten the dough into a 6 × 5 × ½-inch rectangle and cut into rounds with a 1½-inch biscuit cutter.

Place the biscuits on the buttered cookie sheet and convection-bake for 15 to 20 minutes, or until the biscuits are a light brown.

Yield: Approximately 12 biscuits

CHEESE BISCUITS ·

3 ounces Roquefort or blue cheese
1 ounce cream cheese, softened
2 tablespoons butter, softened
2 tablespoons light cream
1 egg, beaten
1 cup all-purpose flour

In a small mixing bowl, blend the cheeses, butter, and cream. Stir in the egg. Turn onto a board covered with ½ cup of the flour. Knead in the flour, then chill several hours.

Preheat the convection oven to 350 degrees for 5 to 10 minutes. Butter a cookie sheet.

Roll out the dough on a board sprinkled with the remaining flour. Cut the dough into 2-inch rounds, place on the buttered cookie sheet, and convection-bake for 8 to 10 minutes, or until lightly browned.

Yield: Approximately 12 biscuits

HONEY-WHEAT BREAD

1 package (¼ ounce) active dry yeast
½ cup lukewarm milk (105 to 115 degrees)
¼ teaspoon granulated sugar
2 tablespoons melted butter
2 tablespoons honey
1 egg, beaten
2 cups all-purpose flour
1 teaspoon salt
1 cup whole-wheat flour

Sprinkle the yeast over the warm milk, then add the sugar and stir to dissolve. Allow to stand about 5 to 8 minutes; the mixture should bubble and grow. If it does not, the yeast is dead; begin again.

In a large mixing bowl, combine the yeast mixture, butter, honey, and egg. Add the salt, then add the flour, 1 cup at a time, mixing until combined. Knead on a lightly floured board until the dough is smooth and elastic, about 10 minutes.

Place the dough in a lightly greased bowl. Cover and allow to rise in a warm, draft-free place for 2 hours, or until doubled in bulk.

Punch the dough down and knead several times, then form into a loaf and place in a well-buttered 8½ × 4½ × 2½-inch loaf pan. Cover and allow to rise again for about 1 hour.

Preheat the convection oven to 325 degrees for 5 to 10 minutes.

Convection-bake the bread for 35 to 40 minutes, or until nicely browned.

Yield: 1 loaf

CUBAN BREAD

If you like a really crusty bread, you'll love this! The crust becomes even crustier because the bread is baked in an oven that has not been preheated, with a pan of hot water placed on the oven floor.

1 package (¼ ounce) active dry yeast
1¼ cups lukewarm water (105 to 115 degrees)
½ teaspoon granulated sugar
1 teaspoon salt
3 to 3½ cups all-purpose flour

Dissolve the yeast in ½ cup of the water, then add the sugar and stir. Allow to stand about 5 to 8 minutes; the mixture should bubble and grow. If it does not, the yeast is dead; begin again.

In a large mixing bowl, combine the yeast mixture and the remaining water. Add the salt and then the flour, 1 cup at a time, mixing well until all the flour is incorporated. Knead on a lightly floured board until smooth and elastic, about 8 to 10 minutes.

Place the dough in a lightly buttered bowl, then cover and allow to rise in a warm, draft-free place for 2 hours, or until doubled in bulk.

Punch the dough down and knead several times, then form into a round loaf and place on a cookie sheet sprinkled with cornmeal. Cover and allow to rise until almost doubled in bulk, about 1½ hours.

Place a pan of hot water on the floor of the convection oven. Cut three slits in the top of the loaf, then place the bread in the oven, on a rack over the hot water. Convection-bake in a 350-degree oven for 35 to 40 minutes, or until the crust is nicely browned.

Yield: 1 loaf

CORN RYE BREAD

1 package (¼ ounce) active dry yeast
Pinch of sugar
¼ cup lukewarm water (105 to 115 degrees)
1 cup very hot water
4 tablespoons (½ stick) butter
1 teaspoon salt
¼ cup firmly packed brown sugar
2 tablespoons dark corn syrup
2 cups rye flour
2 cups all-purpose flour, more if necessary
½ cup cornmeal
2 teaspoons caraway seeds

Dissolve the yeast and sugar in the lukewarm water. Allow the yeast to stand for 5 to 10 minutes, or until it begins to bubble and grow. If it does not, the yeast is dead; begin again.

In a small bowl, combine the hot water, butter, salt, sugar, and corn syrup. In a large bowl, combine the flours, cornmeal, and caraway seeds. Add the yeast and liquid mixtures to the flour and mix with an electric mixer or wooden spoon until a ball can be formed.

Turn the dough out on a lightly floured board and knead for about 10 minutes, or until the dough is smooth and elastic, adding more all-purpose flour if necessary. Place the dough in a lightly buttered bowl, cover, and allow to rise in a draft-free place for about 1½ hours, or until doubled in bulk.

Punch the dough down and knead several times, then form into a ball and place on a lightly buttered cookie sheet. Allow to rise again for 1 hour, or until doubled in bulk.

Preheat the convection oven to 350 degrees for 5 to 10 minutes.

Convection-bake the bread for 35 to 45 minutes, or until the loaf sounds hollow when tapped with a knife and the top is well browned.

Yield: 1 loaf

PUMPERNICKEL RAISIN BREAD

1 package (¼ ounce) active dry yeast
1¼ cups lukewarm water (105 to 115 degrees)
Pinch of sugar
¼ cup molasses
¼ cup firmly packed brown sugar
¼ cup vegetable oil
1 teaspoon salt
1½ cups rye flour
2 cups all-purpose flour, more as needed
½ cup raisins

Dissolve the yeast in ¼ cup of the lukewarm water. Add the sugar and allow to stand for 5 to 10 minutes; the mixture should begin to bubble and grow. If it does not, the yeast is dead; begin again.

In a small bowl, combine the molasses, brown sugar, oil, and remaining water. In a large bowl, combine the salt, flours, and raisins. Add the yeast and liquid mixtures to the flour, then mix with an electric mixer or wooden spoon until a ball can be formed.

Turn the dough out on a lightly floured board and knead for about 10 minutes, or until the dough is smooth and elastic, adding more all-purpose flour as needed. Place the dough in a lightly buttered bowl, cover, and allow to rise in a draft-free place for about 1½ hours, or until doubled in bulk.

Punch the dough down and knead several times, then shape into a loaf and fit into an 8½ × 3½ × 1½-inch loaf pan. Allow to rise again for about 1 hour, or until doubled in bulk.

Preheat the convection oven to 350 degrees for 5 to 10 minutes.

Convection-bake the bread for 35 to 45 minutes, or until the loaf sounds hollow when tapped with a knife and the top is well browned.

Yield: 1 loaf

COTTAGE CHEESE BREAD

1 package (¼ ounce) active dry yeast
¼ cup lukewarm water (105 to 115 degrees)
2 tablespoons plus ¼ teaspoon sugar
1 cup cottage cheese, heated to lukewarm
1 tablespoon grated onion
2 tablespoons butter, melted
1 teaspoon salt
¼ teaspoon baking soda
1 egg
2 to 2½ cups all purpose-flour

Sprinkle the yeast over the water. Add the ¼ teaspoon sugar and stir to dissolve. Allow to stand for about 5 minutes; the mixture should bubble and grow. If it does not, the yeast is dead; begin again.

In a large mixing bowl, combine the cottage cheese, 2 tablespoons sugar, the onion, butter, salt, baking soda, and egg. Stir the softened yeast into the cottage cheese mixture, then gradually incorporate the flour, using an electric mixer, until you have a moderately stiff dough.

Cover the dough and let it rise in a warm place until doubled in bulk, about 2 hours.

Stir the dough down and turn into a well-buttered 2-quart ovenproof casserole. Cover and let rise again until doubled in bulk, about 1 to 1½ hours.

Preheat the oven to 350 degrees for 5 to 10 minutes.

Convection-bake the bread for 30 to 40 minutes, or until the top sounds hollow when tapped with a knife.

Yield: 1 loaf

13
CAKES, COOKIES, AND OTHER DESSERTS

CAKES, COOKIES, AND OTHER DESSERTS

Summertime Blueberry Tart

Chocolate Cheesecake

Cream Puffs Caramel

Double Chocolate Treats

Jumbo Chocolate Chippers

Meringue Kisses

Pilgrim Squares

Butter Cookies

Nut Tarts for Tea

Holiday Fruitcake

Sweet Potato Cake

Macaroons

Crème Caramel

Judy's Chocolate Sponge Roll

Old-Fashioned Gingerbread

Madeleines à la Batia

Baked Plum Compote with Cognac

Almond and Oatmeal Delights

Easy Brown Sugar Brownies

Hungarian Butter Biscuits

Chocolate Truffle Cake

The convection oven will help you create a cornucopia of wonderful desserts. Everything, from the simplest Easy Brown Sugar Brownie to the richest Chocolate Truffle Cake, can be prepared with this appliance.

Homemade isn't so time consuming any more, and desserts made at home are better—and cheaper—than the store-bought variety. So, make a child happy today with a Jumbo Chocolate Chipper, and delight an adult with a tiny, golden Madeleine cake!

SUMMERTIME BLUEBERRY TART

PASTRY

1½ cups all-purpose flour
2 tablespoons granulated sugar
⅛ teaspoon salt
¼ pound (1 stick) butter
2 to 3 tablespoons ice water

FILLING

3 cups blueberries, fresh or frozen
¾ cup granulated sugar
2 teaspoons lemon juice
3 to 4 tablespoons all-purpose flour
¼ teaspoon ground cinnamon

In a small mixing bowl, combine flour, sugar, and salt. Cut the butter into the flour mixture, using a pastry cutter or two knives, until the particles are the size of small peas. Sprinkle ice water over flour 1 tablespoon at a time, and stir with fork until dough is lightly moistened. Form into a ball and refrigerate for 30 minutes.

Meanwhile, combine all the filling ingredients.

Roll the pastry out on a lightly floured board. Fit into an 8-inch springform pan (the pastry should come up about 2 inches on the sides of the pan). Spoon the filling into the pastry and convection-bake in a 375-degree oven for 30 to 40 minutes, or until the pastry is nicely browned.

Serves: 8

CHOCOLATE CHEESECAKE

2 cups vanilla or chocolate cookie
   crumbs
2 cups granulated sugar
5 tablespoons melted butter
4 eggs, separated
3 packages (8 ounces each) cream cheese
1 cup sour cream
¾ cup unsweetened cocoa
1 teaspoon vanilla extract

Preheat the convection oven to 300 degrees for 5 to 10 minutes.

Combine the cookie crumbs, ¼ cup of the sugar, and the melted butter in a bowl and mix thoroughly. Press the crumbs into the bottom and halfway up the sides of a 9-inch springform pan. Refrigerate until ready to use.

Beat the egg whites until they form soft peaks. Set aside.

In a large bowl, combine the cream cheese and remaining sugar and beat with an electric mixer until creamy. Add the egg yolks, one at a time, beating after each addition. Add the sour cream, cocoa, and vanilla and beat until thoroughly blended.

Gently fold the egg whites into the cheese mixture and pour into the crumb-lined pan. Convection-bake for 50 to 60 minutes or until set, then remove from the oven and keep at room temperature for 1 hour.

Refrigerate for 6 to 8 hours before serving.

Serves: 12

CREAM PUFFS CARAMEL

From the youngest to the oldest, everyone delights at the sight of a cream puff. And a cream puff filled with whipped cream, and then topped with hot caramel sauce, is even more pleasurable. An extra attraction to the person who prepares cream puffs is the fact that they're not really difficult to make. They just look that way.

PASTRY

½ cup water
4 tablespoons (½ stick) butter
½ cup all-purpose flour
Pinch of salt
1 teaspoon granulated sugar
2 eggs, beaten

FILLING

1 cup heavy cream
1 tablespoon granulated sugar
1 teaspoon vanilla extract

SAUCE

4 ounces caramel candies
¼ cup light cream
1 teaspoon vanilla extract

Preheat the convection oven to 325 degrees for 5 to 10 minutes. Butter a cookie sheet.

In a small saucepan, heat the water and butter to boiling. Stir in the flour, salt, and sugar and continue stirring until the mixture leaves the sides of the pan. Remove from the heat and stir in the eggs until the mixture is thoroughly combined.

Using a tablespoon, spoon the puff pastry mixture onto the buttered cookie sheet. You will have 8 puffs. Convection-bake for 20 to 25 minutes, or until the puffs have risen and are golden brown. Remove the puffs from oven and slit the tops to allow steam to escape. Allow the puffs to cool.

Whip the cream with the sugar and vanilla until the cream is thick and whipped. Refrigerate until ready to use.

In the top of double boiler, and over hot water, melt the caramel candies. Gradually stir in the cream and vanilla and cook, stirring occasionally, until the caramel mixture is smooth.

Cut the tops off the puffs and fill each puff with whipped cream. Replace the tops and spoon the caramel sauce over the puffs. Place the puffs in the refrigerator until ready to serve.

Serves: 8

DOUBLE CHOCOLATE TREATS

1 cup all-purpose flour
1 teaspoon baking powder
¼ teaspoon baking soda
¼ teaspoon salt
½ cup unsweetened cocoa
6 ounces (1½ sticks) butter
1½ cups granulated sugar
¼ cup sour cream
2 eggs
1 teaspoon vanilla extract
½ cup semisweet chocolate morsels

Preheat the convection oven to 300 degrees for 5 to 10 minutes. Butter well a 9-inch-square pan.

In a large mixing bowl, combine the flour, baking powder, baking soda, salt, and cocoa and mix well.

In another large bowl, beat the butter, sugar, and sour cream with an electric mixer until creamy. Add the eggs, one at a time, beating after each addition. Beat in the vanilla.

Gradually beat in the flour mixture, and continue beating until all the ingredients are thoroughly combined. Stir in the chocolate morsels.

Spoon the batter into the well-buttered pan and convection-bake for 25 to 30 minutes.

Allow to cool before cutting into squares.

Yield: Approximately 16 squares

JUMBO CHOCOLATE CHIPPERS

1 cup all-purpose flour
½ teaspoon baking soda
½ teaspoon salt
4 tablespoons (½ stick) butter
2 ounces cream cheese
¾ cup firmly packed brown sugar
1 egg
1 teaspoon vanilla extract
1 package (6 ounces) semisweet chocolate morsels

Preheat the convection oven to 300 degrees for 5 to 10 minutes.

In a small bowl, combine flour, baking soda, and salt. In a large bowl, cream the butter and cheese, using an electric mixer. Beat in the sugar. Add the egg and vanilla, and beat until thoroughly combined. Beat in the flour mixture, then stir in the chocolate morsels.

Drop by well-rounded tablespoonfuls onto an ungreased cookie sheet. Convection-bake for 12 to 15 minutes, or until the cookies are golden brown.

Yield: 15 jumbo cookies

MERINGUE KISSES

2 egg whites
⅛ teaspoon salt
¼ teaspoon cream of tartar
1 teaspoon vanilla extract
¾ cup granulated sugar
½ cup chopped walnuts

Preheat the convection oven to 225 degrees for 5 to 10 minutes.

In a large mixing bowl, using an electric mixer, beat the egg whites, salt, cream of tartar, and vanilla at high speed until soft peaks are formed. Add the sugar, 1 tablespoon at a time, and continue beating until stiff, glossy peaks can be formed with a spoon. Fold in the nuts.

Drop the mixture by rounded teaspoonfuls onto the buttered cookie sheet and convection-bake for 35 to 45 minutes, or until the meringue peaks begin to brown and the meringues are dry.

Yield: Approximately 24 meringue kisses

Variations: Substitute chocolate morsels or chopped dates for the nuts.

PILGRIM SQUARES

CRUST

1 cup graham-cracker crumbs
¼ cup melted butter
½ teaspoon ground cinnamon

FILLING

1½ cups cooked, pureed pumpkin (may be canned)
1 cup applesauce
½ cup firmly packed brown sugar
1 teaspoon ground cinnamon
½ teaspoon freshly grated nutmeg
⅛ teaspoon ground ginger
2 teaspoons all-purpose flour
2 eggs, beaten
1 cup light cream

Combine all the ingredients for the crust. Press into the bottom and halfway up the sides of an 8-inch-square pan. Refrigerate until used.

Combine all the filling ingredients and turn into the crumb-lined pan. Convection-bake in a 325-degree oven for 40 to 50 minutes, or until a knife inserted 1 inch from the center comes out dry.

Cut into squares, and serve warm or cooled. Refrigerate leftovers.

Yield: Approximately 16 squares

BUTTER COOKIES

½ pound (2 sticks) butter
¾ cup granulated sugar
1 teaspoon vanilla extract
1¾ cups all-purpose flour

Preheat the convection oven to 300 degrees for 5 to 10 minutes.

In a large mixing bowl, cream the butter and sugar with an electric mixer. Add the vanilla, then mix in the flour until thoroughly combined. Drop by heaping teaspoonfuls onto an ungreased cookie sheet and convection-bake for 10 to 12 minutes, or until the edges begin to brown.

Yield: Approximately 2½ dozen cookies

Variation: Add ½ cup finely chopped nuts, coconut, raisins or gumdrops to batter and bake as directed.

LEMON OR ORANGE BUTTER COOKIES

Decrease the vanilla in the preceding recipe to ½ teaspoon and add ½ teaspoon lemon or orange extract, plus 2 teaspoons grated lemon or orange rind.

NUT TARTS FOR TEA

1 cup all-purpose flour
⅛ teaspoon salt
4 tablespoons (½ stick) butter
1 package (3 ounces) cream cheese
1 to 2 tablespoons ice water
2 eggs, lightly beaten
1½ teaspoons vanilla extract
1½ cups granulated sugar
2 cups walnuts, chopped

In a small mixing bowl, combine the flour and salt. Cut the butter and cream cheese into the flour, using a pastry blender or two knives, until the particles are the size of small peas. Sprinkle ice water over the flour mixture, 1 tablespoon at a time, mixing with a fork until the dough is lightly moistened. Form the dough into a ball and chill for 30 minutes.

Meanwhile, combine the remaining ingredients. Preheat the convection oven to 325 degrees for 5 to 10 minutes.

Roll out the chilled dough on a lightly floured board and cut into 3-inch rounds. Line muffin tins, custard cups, or tart pans with the pastry and fill three-quarters full with the egg-nut mixture. Convection-bake for 20 to 25 minutes, or until the pastry and filling are lightly browned.

Yield: Approximately 18 tarts

HOLIDAY FRUITCAKE

1½ cups all-purpose flour
1¼ teaspoons baking powder
½ teaspoon salt
2 cups mixed candied fruit
½ cup candied cherries
½ cup candied pineapple chunks
½ cup raisins
½ cup firmly packed brown sugar
¼ cup pineapple juice
¼ cup orange juice
½ cup vegetable oil
3 eggs

Preheat the convection oven to 275 degrees for 5 to 10 minutes. Butter and flour a 9 × 5 × 3-inch loaf pan.

Combine the flour, baking powder, and salt in a large mixing bowl. Add the remaining ingredients, mixing well to combine. Pour the batter into the prepared loaf pan and convection-bake for 1 to 1¼ hours, or until a tester inserted in the center of the loaf comes out dry.

Yield: 1 loaf

SWEET POTATO CAKE

2½ cups all-purpose flour
2 teaspoons baking powder
1 teaspoon ground cinnamon
½ teaspoon salt
¼ teaspoon ground ginger
¼ teaspoon freshly grated nutmeg
½ pound (2 sticks) butter, softened
2 cups granulated sugar
5 eggs, separated
½ cup water
1 can (16 ounces) sweet potatoes, drained and mashed
½ cup finely chopped pecans
½ teaspoon vanilla extract
½ teaspoon cream of tartar

Preheat the convection oven to 325 degrees for 5 to 10 minutes. Butter and flour a 10-inch bundt pan.

Combine the flour, baking powder, cinnamon, salt, ginger, and nutmeg. Set aside.

In a large mixing bowl, beat together the butter and sugar at medium speed until light and fluffy. Add the egg yolks, one at a time, beating well after each addition. Add the flour in three additions and the water in two, beginning and ending with the flour, blending thoroughly after each addition. Stir in the sweet potatoes, pecans, and vanilla.

In a large mixing bowl, beat the egg whites and cream of tartar at high speed until the whites are stiff but not dry. Gently fold the whites into the yolk-flour mixture, then pour into the prepared bundt pan and convection-bake for 45 to 55 minutes, or until a tester inserted in the center comes out dry.

Serves: 10 to 12

MACAROONS

3 egg whites
¼ teaspoon salt
¼ teaspoon cream of tartar
½ cup granulated sugar
1 teaspoon vanilla extract
1½ cups (3½-ounce can) flaked coconut

Preheat the convection oven to 275 degrees for 5 to 10 minutes. Butter and flour a cookie sheet.

In a large mixing bowl, beat the egg whites, salt, and cream of tartar at high speed until foamy. Add the sugar, 1 tablespoon at a time, beating constantly until the sugar is dissolved and the whites are glossy and stand in soft peaks. Beat in the vanilla; fold in the coconut.

Drop the macaroons by rounded tablespoonfuls onto the prepared cookie sheet and convection-bake for 15 to 20 minutes, or until lightly browned.

Cool slightly before removing to wire racks.

Yield: Approximately 30 macaroons

CRÈME CARAMEL

1 cup granulated sugar
3 eggs plus 3 egg yolks
2 cups milk, heated until very warm
1 teaspoon vanilla extract

Preheat the convection oven to 325 degrees for 5 to 10 minutes.

In a small saucepan over medium heat, cook ½ cup of the sugar, stirring constantly, until melted and deep golden brown. Remove from the heat and immediately pour 1 tablespoon melted sugar into each of 6 six-ounce custard cups.

Blend together the eggs, egg yolks, and remaining ½ cup sugar. Gradually stir in the milk. Blend in the vanilla, then pour into the prepared custard cups and set the cups in a large baking pan. Put the pan on the rack in the oven, then pour very hot water into the pan to within ½ inch of the top of the custard. Convection-bake for 45 to 50 minutes, or until a knife inserted near the center comes out dry.

Remove the cups promptly from the hot water. Let stand for 5 to 10 minutes at room temperature, then loosen the custard from the cups at the sides with a spatula and invert onto serving plates.

Serves: 6

JUDY'S CHOCOLATE SPONGE ROLL

6 eggs, separated
½ teaspoon cream of tartar
¼ teaspoon salt
¼ cup unsweetened cocoa
1 cup confectioners sugar, plus extra for sprinkling
1 teaspoon vanilla extract
¾ cup all-purpose flour
1 pint heavy sweet cream, whipped with sugar to taste

Preheat the convection oven to 350 degrees for 5 to 10 minutes. Grease a 15½ × 10½ × 1-inch jelly-roll pan. Line the bottom with waxed paper and grease again, then set aside.

Beat the egg whites with the cream of tartar and salt until stiff but not dry. Set aside.

Combine the cocoa and confectioners sugar. Set aside.

Beat the egg yolks until thick and lemon colored. Gradually beat in the cocoa-confectioners sugar mixture. Stir in the vanilla, then gradually fold in the flour.

Gently fold the beaten egg whites into the yolk-flour mixture, then pour the batter into the prepared pan and convection-bake for 18 to 20 minutes, or until the cake springs back when touched gently with a finger.

Place a dish towel on your table or counter. Cover with waxed paper and sprinkle confectioners sugar on the paper. Carefully loosen the cake from the sides of the pan and invert on the waxed paper. Gently pull the waxed paper off the bottom of the cake, then carefully roll up the cake, jelly-roll fashion (from one long side), rolling the sugared paper up with the cake. Wrap in a towel and allow to cool for 30 minutes.

Unroll the cake very gently, remove the waxed paper, and spread with the whipped cream. Reroll and chill until serving time.

Serves: 8

OLD-FASHIONED GINGERBREAD

2 eggs, lightly beaten
¾ cup dark molasses
¾ cup firmly packed dark brown sugar
¾ cup melted butter
1 teaspoon ground ginger
1 teaspoon ground cinnamon
2 teaspoons baking soda
½ teaspoon baking powder
¼ teaspoon salt
2⅓ cups all-purpose flour
1 cup boiling water

Preheat the convection oven to 300 degrees for 5 to 10 minutes. Butter a 9-inch-square pan.

In a large mixing bowl, combine the eggs with the molasses, brown sugar, and butter. Combine all the dry ingredients and stir gradually into the egg mixture. Mix thoroughly, then add the boiling water and mix again, making sure all the ingredients are thoroughly combined.

Spoon the gingerbread batter into the buttered pan and bake for 40 to 45 minutes, or until a toothpick inserted in the center comes out dry.

Serve hot, with whipped cream or vanilla ice cream.

Serves: 8

MADELEINES À LA BATIA

Marcel Proust, the French novelist, ate a small, scallop-shaped cake one afternoon while having tea with his mother. The cake unleashed a flood of memories, and Proust went on to write *Remembrance of Things Past.* Today not everyone reads Proust, but everyone seems to like the little scalloped cakes that inspired him. There are many recipes for madeleines, and here's one easy version.

2 eggs
⅛ teaspoon salt
⅓ cup granulated sugar
½ teaspoon vanilla extract
½ cup all-purpose flour
¼ cup melted butter

Preheat the convection oven to 350 degrees. Butter and flour two madeleine tins (each tin holds 12 madeleines).

Beat the eggs with salt. Add the sugar gradually, beating until the mixture is stiff, then add the vanilla. Gradually add the flour to the egg mixture and stir until well combined. Add the butter gradually, stirring constantly.

Fill the madeleine tins about three-quarters full and convection-bake for 8 to 10 minutes, or until brown.

Yield: Approximately 24 madeleines

BAKED PLUM COMPOTE WITH COGNAC

The French preserve plums, green and purple and yellow, in liqueurs or cognac. In this recipe, small purple plums are baked with Cognac. The result? A delicious compote that can be served by itself as a dessert, or spooned over vanilla ice cream. Call it a relish, if you wish, and serve it as a side dish with roast pork, goose, or duck.

3-inch strip lemon peel
1 pound purple plums (also known as Italian plums)
¼ cup granulated sugar
½ cup orange juice
¼ cup Cognac
½ teaspoon ground cinnamon

Place the lemon peel in a 350-degree convection oven and allow to dry for 10 minutes.

Cut the plums in half and remove the pits, then place the fruit in an ovenproof casserole. Stir in the sugar, orange juice, Cognac, and cinnamon and mix gently. Add the lemon peel.

Cover and convection-bake in a 350-degree oven for 10 to 15 minutes, then remove from the oven and taste the syrup. Correct the seasoning, adding more sugar or orange juice if you wish, and bake an additional 5 minutes, uncovered.

Serve hot or cold.

Serves: 4 to 6

ALMOND AND OATMEAL DELIGHTS

1¼ cups all-purpose flour
1 teaspoon baking soda
1 teaspoon salt
1 cup granulated sugar
1 cup firmly packed light brown sugar
½ pound (2 sticks) butter, softened
2 eggs
1 teaspoon almond extract
1 cup slivered blanched almonds
3 cups quick-cooking oats

Combine the flour, soda, and salt in a small bowl. In a large bowl, cream together the sugars, butter, eggs, and almond flavoring, beating until fluffy. Gradually stir in the flour mixture. Add the almonds and oats, making sure all the ingredients are thoroughly combined. Form the dough into a roll and refrigerate for 2 hours.

Preheat the convection oven to 300 degrees for 5 to 10 minutes.

Slice the dough into thin rounds and place on an ungreased cookie sheet. Bake for 8 to 10 minutes.

Yield: Approximately 50 cookies

EASY BROWN SUGAR BROWNIES

These brownies are a child's delight—especially so if you let the child help you make them. It's so easy the kids in your house will do it without your help the next time. Just instruct them about the safety dos and don'ts of convection cooking.

1 cup firmly packed light brown sugar
¼ cup melted butter
1 egg, beaten
¾ cup all-purpose flour
1 teaspoon baking powder
½ teaspoon salt
½ teaspoon vanilla extract
½ cup chopped, blanched almonds

Combine the sugar and butter. Stir in the egg, then add the flour, baking powder, and salt. Mix thoroughly, then stir in the vanilla and almonds.

Spoon the batter into a buttered, 8-inch-square pan and convection-bake in a 300-degree oven for 25 to 30 minutes, or until a knife inserted in the center comes out dry. Cool before cutting into squares.

Yield: Approximately 18 brownies

HUNGARIAN BUTTER BISCUITS

3 cups all-purpose flour
½ pound (2 sticks) butter
4 egg yolks
½ cup granulated sugar
½ teaspoon salt
1 egg, beaten

Mix the flour and butter with a pastry blender, or two knives, until the mixture forms crumbs about the size of small peas. Add the 4 egg yolks, sugar, and salt and work the mixture together. Knead for a minute or so, then roll the dough into a ball and refrigerate overnight.

Preheat the convection oven to 300 degrees for 5 to 10 minutes.

On a floured board, roll out the dough into a sheet 1 inch thick. Cut into rounds with a biscuit or cookie cutter, then score the tops of the biscuits, using a knife, and brush with beaten egg.

Place the biscuits on a cookie sheet and convection-bake for 20 to 25 minutes, or until golden brown and firm in the middle.

Cool before serving.

Yield: 12 to 15 biscuits

CHOCOLATE TRUFFLE CAKE

2 cups milk
1½ cups granulated sugar
½ pound bitter chocolate
½ pound (2 sticks) butter
4 eggs, separated
2½ cups all-purpose flour
2 teaspoons baking powder

In a 2-quart saucepan, combine the milk, sugar, chocolate, and butter and bring to a boil. Allow the mixture to cool.

Preheat the convection oven to 300 degrees for 5 to 10 minutes. Butter well a 2½-quart ovenproof cake mold.

Pour the chocolate mixture into a large bowl. Gradually beat in the egg yolks and then the flour and baking powder. Beat for 5 minutes by hand, or for 2 minutes with an electric mixer.

Beat the egg whites until stiff and fold into chocolate mixture, then pour the mixture into the well-buttered cake mold and convection-bake for 45 to 55 minutes. (The center of this dessert will be moist, not firm or dry.)

Cool for 10 minutes and remove to a rack. Cool before serving.

Serves: 10 to 12

14
THE NEWEST AND OLDEST WAY OF PRESERVING FOODS: DEHYDRATION

THE NEWEST AND OLDEST WAY OF PRESERVING FOODS

Argentine Puchero

Swiss Pear and Potato Casserole

Zucchini-Dill Bread

Easy Dinner Rolls

Fruit Compote

Fruit 'n' Custard Pie

Southern-Style Fried Apple Pies

Best Apricot Jam

Apricot Leather or Apricot Jerky

Herb Salt

Herb Mustard

Herb Butter

Dehydrating is one of the oldest ways of preserving foods. Indians and America's pioneers alike dehydrated herbs, vegetables, and meats as a way of preserving them for long winter months. In Switzerland today home-dried fruits and meat are still a part of the cuisine.

Some of today's convection ovens have dehydration features. This means that the thermostat can be turned down to 140 degrees, while the timer allows the food to dehydrate for the many hours needed for this process. The convection ovens that have the dehydration feature also have special racks that should be used while processing food through dehydration.

Some interesting advantages to dehydrated foods are:

• They take up very little storage space.

• They require no freezing or refrigeration.

• The cost of dehydrating in a convection oven is very low, because the temperature used is very low. An energy saver!

• Dehydrated fruits make marvelous snacks—there are no empty calories in dried apricots or apple slices.

• Summer vegetables, when dehydrated, make an excellent addition to winter's soups and stews.

• If you, or anyone you know, likes to go camping, dehydrated foods are light in weight. Perfect for the backpacker.

If your convection oven has a dehydration feature, read the manufacturer's directions carefully, and follow them.

The United States Department of Agriculture also has the following hints when dehydrating foods:

• Use only the freshest and ripest fruits and vegetables. Avoid overripe produce—they could either be tough or have a mushy texture.

• Wash and clean all produce thoroughly before proceeding with dehydration.

• Blanch vegetables before dehydrating. You may also prefer to blanch light-colored fruits to prevent darkening during drying and storing.

• Cool all dehydrated foods before packing, and pack foods into clean, dry containers that are waterproof and that can be tightly sealed.

• Package dehydrated foods in small quantities, so that when you open a package all the contents can be used soon after.

• Dehydrated foods should be stored in a cool, dark, dry place. If moisture gets to food, it might become moldy. Throw out any food that has mold, a strange color, or an unpleasant odor.

• Dehydrated food can be reconstituted by cooking, soaking, or a combination of the two methods.

• One cup of dried fruit reconstitutes to 1½ cups. One cup of dried vegetables reconstitutes to approximately 2 cups.

ARGENTINE PUCHERO

2 pounds beef short ribs
½ cup dehydrated tomato leather, cut into pieces
1 tablespoon dehydrated onion
¼ cup dehydrated carrots
¼ cup dehydrated celery
½ cup dehydrated corn
½ dehydrated green pepper
1 clove garlic, peeled and mashed
½ teaspoon dehydrated dill weed
Salt and freshly ground black pepper to taste
1 cup cooked chick-peas
2 potatoes, peeled and cubed

Place all the ingredients except for the chick-peas and potatoes in a large soup pot or Dutch oven. Add water to cover, then cover and cook for 2 hours, or until the meat is tender.

Add the chick-peas and potatoes and cook for another 30 minutes, or until the potatoes are tender.

Variation: If you wish, you can convection slow-cook the *puchero.* Place all the ingredients in a 3-quart ovenproof casserole. Cover and convection slow-cook at 225 to 250 degrees for 6 to 8 hours, or until the meat is tender.

Serves: 6

SWISS PEAR AND POTATO CASSEROLE

1 cup dehydrated pear slices
2 tablespoons butter
1 onion, peeled and chopped
3 potatoes, peeled and cubed
Salt and freshly ground black pepper to taste
¼ teaspoon ground cinnamon

Soak the pear slices in water for 2 hours. Drain.

Heat the butter in a large skillet. Sauté the onion, stirring, until transparent, then add all other ingredients to the skillet and add water to cover.

Cover and cook over low heat for 30 to 40 minutes, or until the potatoes and pear slices are tender.

Serves: 4

ZUCCHINI-DILL BREAD

1 cup shredded, dehydrated zucchini
2 tablespoons dehydrated dill weed
2 cups boiling water
¼ pound (1 stick) butter
¾ cup granulated sugar
1 teaspoon vanilla extract
3 eggs, lightly beaten
2 cups all-purpose flour
½ teaspoon salt
1 teaspoon baking powder
1 teaspoon baking soda
¼ teaspoon ground cardamon

Combine the zucchini and dill. Pour the boiling water over all, and let stand for 1 hour.

Preheat the convection oven to 300 degrees for 5 to 10 minutes. Butter an 8½ × 4½ × 2½-inch loaf pan.

Cream together the butter and sugar. Stir in the vanilla. Gradually add the eggs, then continue beating until everything is thoroughly combined.

Gradually add the flour, salt, baking powder, baking soda, and cardamon. Mix thoroughly. Drain the zucchini and dill and add to the bread mixture. Beat thoroughly.

Spoon the batter into the buttered loaf pan and convection-bake for 45 to 50 minutes, or until a knife inserted into the loaf comes out dry.

Yield: 1 loaf

EASY DINNER ROLLS

1 can refrigerator biscuits
2 teaspoons grated dehydrated lemon peel
2 tablespoons melted butter

Separate the biscuits and stretch each one out, until it is approximately 5 inches long.

Combine the lemon peel and butter and brush on each roll. Twist each roll, then place on a cookie sheet and convection-bake in a 375-degree oven for 10 to 15 minutes, or until the rolls are brown.

Yield: 10 rolls

FRUIT COMPOTE

2 cups dehydrated apricots
1 cup dehydrated pear slices
1 cup dehydrated apple slices
Juice of ½ lemon, or more to taste
¼ teaspoon ground cinnamon
½ cup granulated sugar, or more to taste

Place all the ingredients in a large saucepan and cover with water. Cover the saucepan and cook until the fruits are tender and the juice and water have combined to form a light syrup. Add more sugar or lemon, if you wish.

May be served hot or cold.

Serves: 6

Variation: If you wish, the compote can also be prepared in the convection oven, by slow cooking. Use an ovenproof 2-quart casserole. Cover and convection slow-cook at 225 to 250 degrees for 3 to 4 hours, or until the fruits are tender.

FRUIT 'N' CUSTARD PIE

1 nine-inch pie shell, partially baked (see page 125)
5 each dehydrated peaches, apricots, and plums
1 cup heavy sweet cream
2 tablespoons light brown sugar
3 eggs, lightly beaten
Pinch of salt
1 teaspoon grated dehydrated orange peel
1 teaspoon ground cinnamon
Pinch of freshly grated nutmeg

Preheat the convection oven to 350 degrees for 5 to 10 minutes.

Place the dehydrated fruits in the pie shell. Combine all the other ingredients and beat until blended. Pour over the fruits in the crust and convection-bake for 25 to 35 minutes, or until a knife inserted in the center comes out dry.

Serves: 6

SOUTHERN-STYLE FRIED APPLE PIES

2 cups all-purpose flour
½ teaspoon salt
½ teaspoon baking soda
½ cup vegetable shortening
1 tablespoon vinegar
4 to 5 tablespoons cold water
1 cup dehydrated apple slices
½ teaspoon ground cinnamon
1 teaspoon grated dehydrated lemon
   peel
Fat for deep frying

Combine the flour, salt, and baking soda. With a pastry blender or two knives, cut the shortening into the flour until the particles are the size of small peas. Gradually add the vinegar and water until the dough is moist. Form into a ball and chill for 30 minutes.

Combine the apples, cinnamon, and lemon peel in a saucepan. Add water to cover and simmer until the apples are tender, then drain and chop the apples into small pieces. Allow the filling to cool.

On a floured board, roll out the dough and cut into approximately 15 four-inch squares. Put 1 tablespoon of filling on half of each square. Moisten the edges and fold the pastry squares in half, forming a triangle. Seal the edges and chill for 30 minutes.

Deep-fry the pies in 375-degree fat until light brown. Drain and serve warm.

Yield: Approximately 15 fried pies

BEST APRICOT JAM

1½ cup dehydrated apricots
Water
  1 cup granulated sugar, or more to taste

Place the apricots in a large saucepan. Cover with water and cook over low heat until the apricots are tender. Allow the apricots to cool in the cooking water.

Puree the apricots, with the water, in a food processor or a food mill. Return the apricot puree to the saucepan and cook, over very low heat. Add the sugar gradually, then stir and taste. (This jam is best if slightly tart.)

Cook, uncovered, for 30 to 45 minutes, or until the jam is thick. Test by placing a spoonful of jam on a plate and placing the plate in refrigerator. The jam should be thick after 5 minutes.

Spoon the jam into sterilized jars and store in the refrigerator.

Yield: Approximately 2 pints

APRICOT LEATHER OR APRICOT JERKY

In the eastern part of the United States, a child's delight is something called "apricot leather" or "shoe leather"—a dried, sweetly sour puree of apricots wrapped in clear plastic that can be bought in candy stores, health food stores, and stores catering to a Mideast clientele. In California, the same delicacy is known as "apricot jerky." With the convection oven's dehydrating process you can make your own—delicious no matter what you call it.

3 pounds soft, ripe apricots, washed, pitted, and cut into pieces
2 tablespoons lemon juice

Using a blender or a food processor, puree the apricots. Add the lemon juice to the puree.

Spoon the puree onto dehydrating racks, which have been covered with plastic wrap, and dehydrate in the convection oven according to manufacturer's directions.

A SCATTERING OF HERBS

Cooking with your own dried herbs can be a very satisfactory experience. You can combine herbs as you wish, creating your own unique melange. Add herbs to salt, mustard, and butter to use in cooking and seasoning.

HERB SALT

2 tablespoons dehydrated basil leaves
2 tablespoons dehydrated parsley
1 tablespoon dehydrated tarragon
1 cup salt

Place the herbs in a blender and crumble at low speed. Gradually add the salt. Blend mixture until the herbs are as fine as the salt.

Pour into a large kitchen shaker.

Yield: Approximately 1 cup

HERB MUSTARD

1 cup Dijon-type mustard
1 teaspoon dehydrated dill, crumbled
1 teaspoon dehydrated thyme, crumbled

Mix the mustard and herbs and spoon into a jar. Cover and refrigerate for 48 hours, to allow the herb flavor to permeate the mustard.

Yield: Approximately 1 cup

HERB BUTTER

Herb butters are delicious whether spread on warm, crusty French bread or used as a topping over hot, cooked vegetables.

¼ pound (1 stick) sweet butter, cut into
    4 to 6 pieces
1 tablespoon dehydrated dill weed
2 tablespoons dehydrated onion

Place the butter in a food processor and gradually add the dill and onion. Process until smooth.

Yield: Approximately 1 cup

Note. Herb butter may also be prepared with an electric hand mixer, or may be mixed with a fork. If using a fork, allow the butter to soften slightly first.

INDEX

Ham puffs, 23
Ham-potato scallop, 96
Hamburgers, stuffed, 33
Herb butter, 168
Herb mustard, 168
Herb salt, 167
Herbed brisket of beef, 61
Herbs, to dry, 167
Honey chicken, 41
Honey-wheat bread, 138
Hot dog kebabs and baked beans, 88
Hungarian butter biscuits, 157
Hungarian stuffed roast chicken, 40

Insulation of convection ovens, 5
Irene's baked acorn squash, 99

Jam, apricot, 166
Jansson's Temptation, traditional, 97
Judy's chocolate sponge roll, 154
Juniper beef stew, 76

Kebabs, 51, 86–88

Lamb, 62–65, 86–88
    and biscuits, 64
    chops, family style, 37
    kabobs, 87, 88
    leg of, roast, 36
    rack of, 37
    shanks, 64, 78
    spareribs, 38
Leeks, Jansson's Temptation, 97
Lemon butter cookies, 150
Lemon soufflé, 115
Lenke's cream cheese pie, 130
Lobster, Herb McCarthy's Bowden Square, 53

Macaroni and cheese, old-fashioned, 108
Macaroni shells and shrimp, 109
Macaroons, 152
Madeleines à la Batia, 155
Meat loaf Wellington, 32
Meat thermometers, 5, 27
Meringue kisses, 149
Mexican chicken molé, 81
Microwave ovens, 4
Molé, chicken, 81
Money saving of convection oven, 3
Moussaka, 63
Muffins, apricot, 134
Mushroom-bacon quiche, 126
Mushrooms, stuffed, 21
Mushrooms, Tuscan veal chops with, 68
Mustard, herb, 168

Noodle pudding, 106
Noodles Budapest, 107
Nut tarts, 131

Oatmeal and almond delights, 156
Olive and tomato pie, 128
Olive tarta Español, 15
Onion soup, 70
Onion tart, French, 18
Orange butter cookies, 150
Orange custard pie, 128
Orange puff pancake, 119
Orzo, baked, and chicken livers, 109

Ossobuco à la Modena, 78
Oxtail stew, 77

Pancakes, puffed, 113, 118–119
Pasta, 105–109
Pastitsio Idra, 106
Pastry shells, 125, 130
Pâté, brandied, 12
Pâte Brisée, 125
Pâté de Campagne, 14
Pâté en croûte, 13
Pâté of goose with pistachios, 15
Pear and potato casserole, 163
Pennsylvania Dutch pancake, 118
Peppers, baked saffron rice with, 94
Peppers, stuffed, 94
Pie crusts, 125
Pilaf of rice, 86
Pilgrim squares, 149
Pineapple pork chops, glazed, 66
Pistachios, pâté of goose with, 15
Pizza, homemade, 127
Plum compote with cognac, 156
Polynesian rumaki, 89
Popovers, 134
Pork:
    and apple casserole, 66
    Cantonese, with stir-fried vegetables, 67
    chops, glazed pineapple, 66
    and potato casserole, 67
    sweet and pungent, 79
Pot roast, piquant, 76
Potage Basquaise, 71
Potato:
    biscuits, 137
    -cheese puffs, 24
    ham and egg hash, 96
    -ham scallop, 96
    Niçoise, 97
    and pear casserole, 163
    and pork casserole, 67
    and spinach mousse, 98
    stuffing, dilled breast of veal with, 39
    twice-baked, 31, 95
Preheating, 27, 28, 123
Proust, Marcel, 159
Puchero, Argentine, 163
Pumpernickel raisin bread, 141
Pumpkin, Pilgrim squares, 149
Pumpkin surprise, 60
Punjabi lamb spareribs, 38

Quiches, 17, 126

Raita, 87
Rice, saffron, with peppers, 94
Rice pilaf, 86
Roast beef dinner, 29
Roast chestnuts, 10
Roasting methods, 27–28
Rock Cornish game hens in cream, 42
Rumaki, Polynesian, 89
Rye corn bread, 140

Saffron rice with peppers, 94
Salmon soufflé, 116
Salmon steaks with cucumber cream, 50
Salt, herb, 167
Sauerbraten, gingery, 59
Sausage bake, 68

Sausage quiches, 17
Scallop kebabs, 89
Scones, 135
Seafood kebabs, 89
Shad, baked, in cream, 52
Shashlik, 85, 86
Short ribs, hot and spicy, 77
Shrimp:
    Creole casserole, 52
    kebabs, 89
    macaroni shells and, 109
    Marbella, 53
Slow-cooking, in convection oven, 5, 75, 76–81
Soufflés, 114–118
South American empañadas, 16
Southern-style fried apple pies, 166
Spaghetti squash, 99
Spinach and potato mousse, 98
Spinach quiche, 126
Split-pea soup Amsterdam, 80
Sponge roll with chicken Mornay, 22
Spoon bread, 135
Squash, see Acorn squash; Spaghetti squash; Zucchini
Stews, 57–71
Stir-fried vegetables, pork with, 67
Striped bass, baked, 50
Strudel, cabbage, 11
Sweet and pungent pork Young China, 79
Sweet potato biscuits, 137
Sweet potato cake, 152
Sweet potato surprise, 98
Swiss pear and potato casserole, 163
Swordfish kebabs with lime, 51
Szalonna, 107

Tart, French onion, 18
Toasted almonds Saratoga, 9
Tokyo seafood kebabs, 89
Tomato and olive pie, 128
Tomatoes, filled, 100
Tomatoes Provençale, 100
Traditional Jansson's Temptation, 97
Tuscan veal chops with mushrooms, 68
Twice-baked potatoes with caviar, 31
Twice-baked potatoes with cheese, 95

Utensils for convection ovens, 5–6, 123

Veal:
    birds, 39
    breast of, with dilled potato stuffing, 39
    chops, with mushrooms, 68
    ossobuco, 78
    shanks, roast, 38
Vegetable and beef stew, 58
Vegetables, 93–102
Vegetables, stir-fried, with pork, 67

Walnut fudge pie, 129
Walnut-apple pie, 129
Walnuts, fettucine with, 108
Wild duck, roast, 46

Ziti casserole, 107
Zucchini, stuffed, 101
Zucchini Florentine, 102
Zucchini with cheese and basil, 101
Zucchini-dill bread, 164